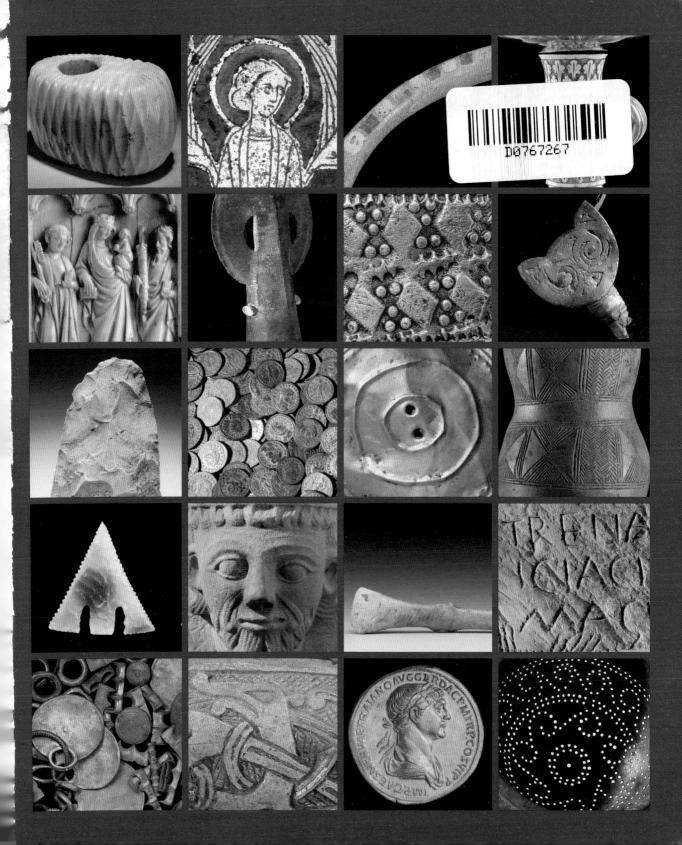

D0767267

Discovered in Time

TREASURES FROM EARLY WALES

First published in 2011 by Amgueddfa Cymru - National Museum Wales,
Cathays Park, Cardiff, CF10 3NP, Wales.

© the National Museum of Wales

ISBN 978 0 7200 0604 9

Editing and production: Mari Gordon
Design: mopublications.com
Printed by: Gomer Press
Available in Welsh as *Canfod y Gymru Gynnar*
ISBN 978 0 7200 0605 6

Amgueddfa Cymru would like to thank the following for permission
to reproduce images: Her Majesty the Queen (p. 142 and preliminaries);
Bibliothèque municipale de Besançon (p. 146); British Library (p. 154);
Cadw (p. 96); Mrs E. Gwynn (p. 146); the Master and Fellows of Corpus
Christi College, Cambridge (p. 136); National Museums Liverpool (left panel,
p. 149); National Museums Scotland (p. 43); Peter Skelly, William May
and Joe Perry (p. 60); Royal Commission on the Ancient and Historical
Monuments of Wales (p. 129); Society of Antiquaries of London (pp. 3, 58).

Discovered in Time

TREASURES FROM EARLY WALES

Edited by Mark Redknap

NATIONAL MUSEUM WALES BOOKS 2011

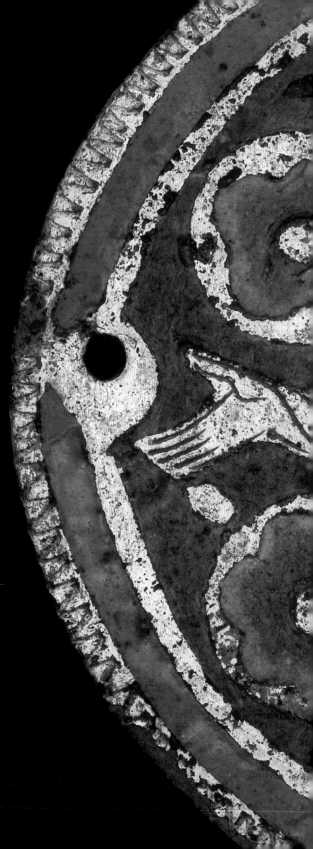

In memory of Edward Lhuyd
(1660-1709)

Antiquary, Celtic scholar, botanist, palaeontologist, cataloguer and faultless organiser of collections, Keeper of the Ashmolean Museum, and instigator of Parochial Enquiries embracing the geography, antiquities and natural history of Wales.

'The first great Welsh Archaeologist'

(Glyn Daniel)

Foreword

The National Museum of Wales came into being with the reawakening of national consciousness in late Victorian and Edwardian times. We have recently seen a second awakening, and some of the aspirations of the early dreamers have been met – we now have an Assembly and a Government for Wales that is itching for more powers and creating the capacity for delivering real devolution to the people who live west of Offa's Dyke.

As it did a century ago, Wales has been experiencing a wave of inward migration. More people are either children of immigrants or themselves immigrants, from across the border or even further afield. Existing inhabitants need to understand the background of incomers, and incomers as well as 'natives' must understand the history and culture of where they now live. However, as this book shows, in Wales there are no 'natives': we are all incomers, and it is only the degree that differs. To me, therefore, this introduction to some of the treasures in our national collections represents a highly accessible way to understand more about the people who have inhabited what is now Wales. The people who made the objects illustrated here were different from us, but not all that different. With just a little effort we can understand their hopes and desires, and respect them all the more.

I cannot recommend too highly this beautifully illustrated book, and the role I foresee it playing in enlightening us, 'native' and 'incomer' alike, about the people who claimed this land of Wales as theirs long before us.

Eurwyn Wiliam, Chairman of the Royal Commission on the Ancient and Historical Monuments of Wales, 2011

Acknowledgements

I am delighted that the curators and conservators of the Archaeology & Numismatics Department have been given an opportunity to communicate the latest thinking about many of the fine objects in the national collections, and to present them to a wider audience. It is a pleasure to thank them for their contributions. As experts in their fields, they have provided fresh contextualization of our rich past in Wales. The work is also indebted to the specialist advice and published work of many colleagues. Suggestions for further reading are provided on pages 158-159.

I would like to express my gratitude to Edward Besly, Kenneth Brassil, Evan Chapman, Sian Iles, John Kenyon, Donald Moore and Eurwyn Wiliam for comments and suggestions; Jim Wild and Kevin Thomas for photography and Jackie Chadwick and Tony Daly for illustrations. Mari Gordon, Head of Publications, responded enthusiastically to the initial book proposal and has seen the book through various stages of production with calm efficiency. I would like in particular to thank Richard Brewer, former Keeper of Archaeology & Numismatics, for his constant encouragement and support during the production of this

Contents

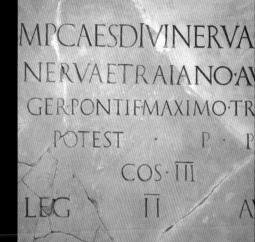

Introduction

COLLECTING VISIONS OF EARLY WALES

Handaxes from the Stopes collection.

This book is about remarkable objects from all over Wales, discoveries from distant times that have been saved from decay and loss and cared for on behalf of the people of Wales.

The objects selected have been arranged in sequence by period and set within their wider cultural and historical contexts. They reflect the creativity of our predecessors and form a mirror of ancient Wales. They belonged to people who lived in Wales hundreds, even thousands of years ago. The purposes behind many of them, and the ways in which successive generations of archaeologists have interpreted them, have changed through time. What were once functional objects are, in some cases, now regarded as works of art or sacred and revered relics. Others have been recycled into objects with new functions and meanings. The lavish decoration on some of the ancient artefacts reflects the aspirations of those who wanted them made, as well as the skills of the people who made them.

So great is the time span between their creation and today, and so complex are the cultural processes involved in their development and use, you might feel they belong to another world, a foreign country. Remarkably, some remained in use until recent times. Others have modern counterparts that perform similar functions. A number have a beauty that appears contemporary, as if made but yesterday. All help to tell the story of life in Wales – in this case, from the arrival of the first hominins 230,000 years ago to the end of the Middle Ages (AD 1530/40s).

'A Shrine of Welsh antiquities'

This was how Lord Pontypridd, the Museum's first President, described the National Museum at its official opening by King George V and Queen Mary in May 1927. The Museum had been years in the making. A national

Art and archaeology
on display in the Main
Hall in 1925 (with the
cast of the 10th-
century Llandough
cross in the alcove).

museum in Wales to satisfy the wish of many 'to acquaint themselves
with the genuine history and antiquities of those people from whom they
are immediately descended' was created long after the establishment of
similar institutions in other countries, and was established by Royal
Charter in 1907. This followed pioneering work by MPs, the Honourable
Society of Cymmrodorion, the Cardiff Naturalists' Society as well as
Cardiff city officials and aldermen from the 1860s and 1870s. The drive for
a national museum gathered momentum from the 1880s, part of the
reawakening of a national consciousness in Wales. By 1903 there were
signs that the campaign for a national museum as a 'storehouse for
Welsh treasures in Wales' could succeed. In 1905 a special committee of
the Privy Council, set up by the government, decreed that there would be
a national museum in Cardiff and a national library in Aberystwyth. The
foundation stone was laid in Cathays Park in 1912, and the western part of
the Main Hall and galleries leading to it were opened to the public in 1922.

The aims of the new multidisciplinary National Museum included the
'complete illustration of the life of man in Wales in the past and today',
within an expanding view of a distinctive identity. At its opening in 1927
Lord Pontypridd referred to the Museum as a 'monument to the Welsh

A cast of the cross from Penmon displayed on the balcony in 1925.

people' and a 'microcosm of the history of the principality'. The inaugural lecture in that year was delivered by Professor (later Sir) John Edward Lloyd in the Reardon Smith Lecture Theatre, and its theme was 'Wales and the past – two voices', meaning those of archaeology and history.

The archaeological collections: discoveries and growth

Collections are central to a museum's work, as is their care and the way in which they are used by the public and by scholars. As with the collections of other disciplines, archaeological and numismatic specimens have been discovered and added in many ways, through a combination of policy, unexpected discovery and good fortune.

Some acquisitions predate the National Museum. In 1912 the collections of the Cardiff Museum & Art Gallery, which had been renamed The Welsh Museum of Natural History, Arts, and Antiquities in 1901 in anticipation of national status, were transferred to the new institution. The Cardiff Museum & Art Gallery had been started in 1868. It had become highly regarded for the rapid growth of its archaeology collections from the 1890s, in particular through the fieldwork of John Ward, who had been appointed Curator in 1893. In 1912 the Museum purchased at a cost of £600 an important collection of tens of thousands of stone tools from Kentish gravel pit sites, formed by the architect, geologist and collector Henry Stopes (1852-1902). The acquisition – negotiated with his daughter, the feminist reformer and pioneer of birth control Dr Marie Stopes (1880-1958) – remains one of the largest single collections of Palaeolithic flint implements from Britain. Reaching Cardiff in 186 packing cases, their aggregate weight was 5 tons!

The benefits of planned collecting are illustrated by one ambitious programme started in 1894 to form a complete collection of casts of early medieval inscribed stones and stone sculpture from Wales. Popularly known as 'early Christian monuments', they formed the most prolific body of material evidence surviving for this period of Welsh history. Created partly to support the efforts to define a distinct Welsh culture within a British context, what made this programme stand out was the systematic approach to cast all known examples – no other country had yet attempted such a project.

The annual casting programme was maintained by the National Museum and only ended because of the Great War, by which time some two-thirds of the known monuments had been cast. These casts were displayed to the public as examples of early Welsh art capable of promoting inspiration among generations of artists, such as T. H. Thomas (1839-1915), known in bardic circles as *Arlunydd Penygarn*. The casts still have great value as an important record of these monuments, especially as some originals have since been lost or damaged.

The new National Museum attracted artefacts from all parts of Wales, including the remarkable Caergwrle bowl, a miniature votive boat of shale, gold and tin donated by Sir Foster Cunliffe (Bart) in 1912 and the great cauldron from Llyn Fawr in Rhondda Cynon Taf, donated by Rhondda Urban District Council in 1913 in return for a replica.

A watercolour by James Basire of the Caergwrle bowl, made shortly after its discovery.

Extending the collections is an important method of enlarging our understanding of a subject. In the case of coins, for example, fresh discoveries can bring examples of new mints or new rulers and moneyers. The rich numismatic collection has grown in importance and standing as a resource for displays and research. Similarly, excavated assemblages have now extended the reference collections of ceramics of all periods, and with them our understanding of their production and patterns of consumption.

Treasure

The treatment of discoveries classed as Treasure has changed considerably over the years, and for the better. Under the old common law of Treasure Trove, since the Middle Ages the right to objects of precious metal found in the soil was claimed by the Crown. In the absence of a national museum, Treasure Trove found in Wales passed initially to the British Museum. Then in 1899 the Cardiff Museum Committee enquired whether Roman gold jewellery that had recently been found at Rhayader in Powys could be deposited in Cardiff 'pending the establishment of a Welsh national museum'. Following the discovery of the Sully hoard of Roman coins and rings in the same year, the British Museum made its selection and the residue was offered to Cardiff Museum for £19 5s 0d. The splitting of this collection fuelled debate and led to further demands for the establishment of a national museum. The first pre-emption of treasure by the National Museum of Wales occurred in 1954, with the acquisition of the Bronze Age gold torcs from Llanwrthwl in Powys.

Under the definitions of the 1996 Treasure Act and its 2002 revision, treasure now includes metallic objects (except coin) over 300 years old with over 10% precious metal, any group of two or more metallic objects of any composition and of prehistoric date and any group of coins over 300 years old (if none are of precious metal, there must be at least 10 of them). The consequent increase in the reporting of certain object types has both enhanced our understanding of poorly documented areas and provided opportunities to strengthen weak parts of the collections – for example, how medieval fashions in Wales reflected those on the Continent and in England. The ability to investigate treasure findspots through fieldwork and excavation has dramatically increased our understanding of discoveries such as the Middle Bronze Age Burton hoard.

Nov² ...BER 15, 1899.

TREASURE TROVE ON SULLY MOOR.

INQUEST AT CARDIFF.

LORD OF THE MANOR'S TITLE.

John Ward at
Tinkinswood
Neolithic tomb.

Scientific research

Fieldwork and excavation provide crucial evidence for interpreting the
past. This allows guesswork or even fiction to be replaced by scientific
observation. In this way, archaeologists can expand the collections into
new areas. In 1912 John Ward became the first Keeper of Archaeology at
the National Museum of Wales. His 1914 excavations at Tinkinswood just
outside Cardiff helped to discredit nineteenth-century interpretations of
these Neolithic tombs as druidical altars. Important excavation archives
have been created that now form the basis of our knowledge of Wales's
unwritten history, such as Goat's Hole Cave in Paviland on the Gower and
the large Neolithic stone-axe quarry at Penmaenmawr in Gwynedd.

Under the leadership of Mortimer Wheeler, who succeeded Ward as
Keeper of Archaeology in 1920, and Cyril Fox, who was Keeper from 1924
to 1926, the Archaeology Department developed a dynamic combination of
collecting, research, excavation, display and publication that continues
today. Wheeler was the first to formulate and control a programme of
research, including the great excavations at the Roman forts of
Segontium near Caernarfon in Gwynedd and Brecon Gaer in Powys.
Following his departure in 1926 to set up the Institute of Archaeology in
London, the planned excavation of the Roman amphitheatre outside the
fortress of the Second Augustan Legion at Caerleon, near Newport, was
largely directed by his wife Tessa and a young lecturer in modern history,
Nowell Myres (later an archaeologist and librarian). With popularizing
flair Wheeler had capitalized on local tradition, which knew the site as
'Arthur's Round Table', to obtain sponsorship from The Daily Mail.

A detail from the reconstruction of the Llan-gors textile - the colour is conjectural.

The Museum has continued to play a key role in the fortress to this day by conducting further excavations and research, notably by Victor Erle Nash-Williams, Keeper of Archaeology from 1926 to 1955.

The Caerleon & Monmouthshire Antiquarian Association, founded in 1847, had set up its own museum of antiquities at Caerleon in 1850. By the 1930s it had realized that it lacked the resources needed to maintain the Museum, so ownership of the building and collections was transferred to the National Museum. In 1987 a new, enlarged museum providing modern display, storage and educational facilities was officially opened. The National Museum also helped create a purpose-built museum in north Wales, a private initiative opened in 1937, on the site of the Roman fort at Segontium in Caernarfon.

The role of fieldwork in pushing the frontiers of knowledge is well illustrated by more recent excavation campaigns, such as the investigations of the Palaeolithic cave at Pontnewydd, Mesolithic Burry Holms on the Gower, the Neolithic axe factory at Mynydd Rhiw in Gwynedd, Bronze and Iron Age Llanmaes in the Vale of Glamorgan, the Roman forum-basilica at Caerwent and of the Viking-age centre at Llanbedrgoch on Anglesey. Excavation at the early medieval royal llys of Llan-gors crannog in Powys produced fragile treasures of a rare and vulnerable kind – waterlogged textiles and worked timber from a range of previously undocumented structures.

New techniques are allowing scholars to draw more information from old material, such as the detailed re-assessment of the Caergwrle bowl, which used X-radiography, geochemical identification, scanning electron microscopy and X-ray diffraction to establish the materials and manufacturing method.

Strategic collection

We also acquire prestigious items in order to save important objects for national heritage – in particular objects found in Welsh soil that are crucial to our understanding of its past. In 2002 a bronze Roman cup with a handle in the form of a leopard was discovered near Abergavenny in Monmouthshire, and reported by the finders under the Portable Antiquities Scheme set up in 1997. Under this scheme thousands of objects from Wales are being recorded each year.

Luck!

One of the most delightful and exciting parts of collecting is the pure serendipity by which a long-lost object can suddenly re-appear or a curator can recognize a misattributed object. In 1901 the Cardiff Museum had purchased a single fourteenth-century ivory diptych leaf that had been found at Llandaff from the estate of John Storrie, for many years Curator of the Museum. In 2007, during preparations for new displays, the missing left-hand leaf showing the Virgin with Child flanked by Saints Peter and Paul was identified in the collections of National Museums Liverpool, and the two devotional scenes were reunited for the first time in centuries.

Such, then, are the diverse ways in which the Museum's archaeological collections and our understanding of them have grown. Revealed, recorded, conserved and displayed by expertise and scholarship, they open up the human past to all. The stories told in this book – seventy out of thousands more – illustrate how we use ancient objects to explore the lives of previous generations. By reuniting the objects with their stories, we can perhaps glimpse a distant collective memory. We can seek and sometimes find a better sense of where we come from, and how our own lives have been shaped.
Mark Redknap

The right-hand leaf of the Llandaff diptych.

Palaeolithic

ABOUT 230,000 TO 9,600 BP

**The handaxe from
Rhossili, Gower.**

The Palaeolithic (Old Stone Age) was a time of changing
climate. Conditions fluctuated from very cold glacials when
ice covered Wales, to warm interglacials such as that of today.
It was against this backdrop of change that our early
ancestors evolved from their African origins and became the
modern humans of today. Most of the evidence for the earliest
human activity in Wales comes from caves. These are found
in areas of Carboniferous limestone in parts of Conwy,
Denbighshire, Gower and south Pembrokeshire.

A handful of stone tools provide evidence for a human
presence in Wales sometime after 700,000 BP (before
present). Chance finds like the handaxe found at Rhossili,
Gower, which fell out of an eroding cliff, are rare.
The only well-preserved site known in Wales is at Pontnewydd
Cave in Denbighshire, where 230,000-year-old early
Neanderthal remains have been found. There is then a long
gap in the archaeological record until the stone tools found at
Coygan Cave in Carmarthenshire, made by true Neanderthals
between 66,000 and 38,000 years ago. These provide a
glimpse of Neanderthals in the landscape of what we now
call Wales.

Early modern humans are first recognized in Wales at the
beginning of the Last Glacial. People like us evolved and were
the first creators of cave paintings at places like Chauvet in
France. They are characterized by the way they made stone
tools by striking blades from carefully prepared cores.

A brown bear
cranium from
Pontnewydd Cave,
Denbighshire.

Blades were also modified into specialized tools for engraving bone or wood, and scrapers for cleaning hides and spear-points. A few sites around Wales have revealed tools typical of this period. Among them is Paviland Cave, Gower, where the 'Red Lady' skeleton was found. At this time the climate was getting colder so animals including mammoth, woolly rhinoceros, brown bear, wolf, arctic fox, reindeer and lemming were present.

If any of the known Welsh caves once contained art, the extreme conditions during the Last Glacial removed the evidence. By 22,000 BP the temperature was so cold that all but the hardiest of life moved south into France and Spain, leaving those southernmost parts of Britain not covered by ice a tundra landscape. About 13,000 BP the climate improved to the extent that vegetation could re-establish itself, enabling herds of deer and horses to enter Britain, followed by people hunting them for food. Their toolkits now included hunting tools such as Cheddar Points, found in Nanna's Cave on Caldey Island in Pembrokeshire. Final Upper Palaeolithic sites including Priory Farm Cave in Pembroke were occupied by people who made tools from local raw materials. This was not the end of the ice cover; about 10,800 BP the climate deteriorated rapidly and led to the development of localized ice on the mountain tops. Humans are again thought to have left Britain, only returning to stay once the climate had improved some years later. Gradually the population increased and as the climate improved they became the hunter-gatherer-fishers of the Early Mesolithic period around 9,600 BP.
Elizabeth A. Walker

1

Teeth from an early Neanderthal child

Pontnewydd Cave, Denbighshire
Lower Palaeolithic: about 230,000 BP
Bone and tooth
Length 25.2mm
Donated by Sir Watkin Williams-Wynn.
NMW acc. nos 83.107H/5.D1740 & D1741

This upper jaw fragment is the largest of just nineteen early Neanderthal fossils discovered during excavations at Pontnewydd Cave. The jaw contains a permanent first molar and a deciduous second molar set in a fragment of bone. The fact that one is a permanent tooth while the other is a milk tooth suggests that the child died when eight or nine years old. The permanent molar shows a characteristic trait of Neanderthals known as taurodontism, the main features of which are an enlarged pulp cavity and coalesced roots.

The remains of at least five individuals have been found in the cave. These people were an early form of Neanderthal who evolved into the true Neanderthals known to have existed later between 115,000 and 30,000 BP.

The sediments that contained the jaw fragment date to around 230,000 years ago. Excavations have revealed a large quantity of stone tools, mostly made of locally available volcanic rocks. These include handaxes, typically used as butchery tools, scrapers for cleaning skins, knives and spear-points. Some butchered animal bones have been found, including a horse bone with evidence for filleting joints of meat and a bear vertebra with cutmarks associated with skinning. Perhaps these early Neanderthals used warm bearskins for clothing.

During the time the early Neanderthals were at Pontnewydd Cave the climate was beginning to deteriorate in an interglacial period around 230,000 BP. The environment was probably open steppe at this time with animals including bears, wolves, rhinoceros, leopards, horses, bison and Norway lemming. The cave was also used by hibernating bears – hence the large number of bear cub milk teeth found in the cave.
EAW

3

A bone spatula

Paviland Cave, Gower, Swansea
Early Upper Palaeolithic: about 29,000 BP
Horse bone
Length 163.7mm
Donated by Miss E. Talbot. NMW acc. no. 15.277/7

This worked bone implement is one of three spatulas discovered at Paviland Cave. It is made of a metapodial – or leg bone – of a horse, and has been carefully carved into this form. What they were used for remains enigmatic; they have two side notches, perhaps for holding a binding, and the rounded edge has a few chips removed from the end. Some theories suggest that they were female figurines, created for a symbolic rather than functional purpose.

The spatula was discovered during the late nineteenth century and was recovered without recording the precise context from which it came. However, it is likely that it was just one of a number of bone, ivory and stone tools found in the cave from which the famous 'Red Lady' skeleton was discovered in 1823 by Professor William Buckland.

The 'Red Lady' skeleton from Paviland Cave is now the oldest dated formal burial known in the British Isles. The skeleton was found in a shallow grave, disturbed by erosion and contained within a mass of iron oxide or ochre. Perforated sea-shell beads and about forty fragments of carved mammoth ivory rods and rings were also found with the burial.

Modern science tells us the 'Red Lady' was actually a 1.7-metres (5 feet 5 inches) tall male in his mid-twenties. He was formally buried in the cave around 29,000 BP and his bones are stained red with ochre, which might have been sprinkled over his body as part of a ritual act or possibly used as a preservative on his clothing. A stone toolkit contains some highly specialized tools, including flint blades modified into scrapers and engraving tools that could have been used to carve the bone spatulas.
EAW

4 Penknife points

Priory Farm Cave, Pembroke, Pembrokeshire
Final Upper Palaeolithic: about 11,800-10,800 BP
Flint
Lengths 58.1mm, 55.4mm, 41.3mm & 37.3mm
Donated by Dr A. Hurrell Style. NMW acc. nos 09.18/4.1, 5.1, 6.1 & 7.1

These four Final Upper Palaeolithic penknife points are made of flint blades retouched along two edges into this distinctive shape. The flint has developed a white patina over the years while buried in the cave. These points could once have been hafted and used as spear points or as knives. They were found in Priory Farm Cave, situated on the valley side of the River Pembroke.

The tools date to between 11,800 and 10,800 BP, a time of temperate conditions during the very end of the Late Glacial interstadial. At this time there was a marked change in the environment, which corresponded with an expansion of birch woodland. People began to make more use of locally available raw materials as the density of woodland increased and mobility became more difficult. The people, therefore, do not appear to have moved around quite as much as they did when they first returned to Britain.
EAW

5

Decorated tooth beads

Kendrick's Cave, Great Orme, Conwy
Final Upper Palaeolithic: about 10,580 BP?
Red deer, deer and auroch teeth
Lengths 44.6mm, 38.6mm, 37.4mm, 49.4mm, 47.3mm, 39.4mm,
39.2mm, 35.6mm & 27.2mm
Donated by Mr F. P. Jowett. NMW acc. nos 80.92H/1-9

These decorated and perforated teeth were discovered during the late
nineteenth century. The teeth, all incisors, comprise six from a large
bovid, probably auroch or wild cattle, one of cervid (deer) and two of red
deer. All the teeth are decorated with a series of incisions on the roots.
All have the remains of, or a complete, perforation towards the base of
the root. This suggests that they were once strung and used as beads.
Some of the incisions still have traces of a red deposit. Red ochre was
used at this time, and it may be there symbolically as decoration.

The cave was first recorded in 1880 shortly after its owner, Thomas
Kendrick, a former copper miner on the Great Orme, expanded his stone-
carving workshop. He showed his finds to a Mr Eskrigge, whose interest
in them led Kendrick to open his cave and his finds to visitors. Also
reportedly found in the cave was a horse upper jaw decorated with a
chevron design, which is now in the British Museum, and four bone
tallies, now in Llandudno Museum.

One of the teeth has been radiocarbon dated. The result is later than
might have been expected, falling in the Late Glacial stadial. The
presence of humans in Wales during this period is unlikely, given the
extreme conditions and open tundra landscape. However, the date of
the tooth, if taken at face value, apparently falls within this very cold
period. New dating now underway will hopefully resolve these
uncertainties.
EAW

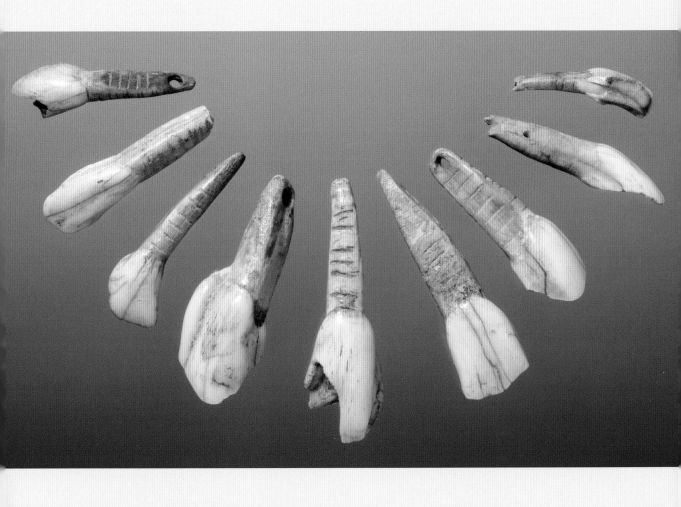

Mesolithic

ABOUT 9,600 TO 6,000 BP

These footprints at Uskmouth are the oldest known human footprints in Wales.

The Mesolithic (Middle Stone Age) was the interlude between the end of the last Ice Age around 9,600 BP and the arrival of the first farmers of the Neolithic around 6,000 BP. As the climate began to improve, vegetation returned and gradually animals and then humans moved back into the British Isles. This heavily wooded landscape was home to red deer, roe deer, wild cattle and pigs, all of which were potential prey for the Mesolithic hunter-gatherer-fishers who lived a seasonally nomadic lifestyle.

People continued to make stone tools using blades, but much smaller ones than previously. The typical tool was the microlith, or stone barb, like those found at Rhuddlan in Denbighshire and on Burry Holms, Gower. These were glued into wooden or antler shafts to make hunting or fishing spears and harpoons.

The sea level at the start of the Mesolithic period was much lower than it is today. As the ice retreated northwards the meltwaters caused this to rise. Today Burry Holms is located on a tidal island, but the Mesolithic campsite would have been situated on a wooded inland hill, overlooking the plain of the River Severn. Adzes, like those found at Trwyn Du on Anglesey, would have been important for clearing trees from areas of land for temporary camps.

Groups of Mesolithic people were highly mobile throughout this period. Indirect evidence for this comes from the decorated pebbles that have so far only been found in Rhuddlan and

A stone adze from Trwyn Du, Anglesey.

Cornwall. Evidence for trade takes the form of the perforated stone beads found at Waun Fignen Felen in Powys, which could have been manufactured in Pembrokeshire at The Nab Head. Communication between groups would have been fairly easy, as people spent part of their year following herds of animals and other important food sources. During the warm summer months they were probably found in inland areas, while in winter they returned to the lower-lying coast or river valleys. These river valleys formed routeways and provided the fish that were an important part of diet at this time. The smaller microliths made during the later Mesolithic, like those found at Short Point in Pembrokeshire, would have been perfect for fishing spears and harpoons.

Excavations at Goldcliff near Newport have discovered not only stone tools, but also the preserved remains of pollen, animal and fish bones. The site now lies in the modern intertidal zone, but during the later Mesolithic (around 6400 BP) it was on a small wooded island with saltmarsh to the seaward side. Shellfish would also have been important in daily diets; the discovery of an antler mattock at Uskmouth, a few kilometers to the west of Goldcliff, suggests that people in this area were digging in the soft muds for seafood such as cockles. However, the most tangible evidence of human presence has been the discovery of their footprints, baked into estuarine clays at both of these sites.
Elizabeth A. Walker

6 A stone bead

Waun Fignen Felen, Powys
Early Mesolithic: about 9,000 BP
Mudstone
Maximum diameter 16.3mm; thickness 2.1mm
Donated by Brecon Beacons National Park. NMW acc. no. 93.39H/227

This stone bead, one of three found, was made from a small disc of water-rolled mudstone. The hole is U-shaped in section, and was drilled from one side only.

Waun Fignen Felen lies in the Upper Swansea Valley. A number of small sites have been found around what was once a Late Glacial lake edge – an ideal spot for hunting. Each of the sites has produced small amounts of flint knapping waste, suggesting that they were locations where people made microliths and other tools for immediate use. Perhaps people came here from the coastal lowlands, ate a meal and stayed overnight before hunting game or waterfowl on the lake. They would then have moved on, taking their food to more permanent camps elsewhere.

Beads had a decorative role. They could have been strung together or sewn onto clothing, but they might also have played a part in a system of exchange. As the beads at Waun Fignen Felen were made of a stone of Pembrokeshire origin, it is possible that these were made at The Nab Head, which is known to have been a bead production centre around 9,000 BP. Among the 700 stone beads found at The Nab Head there were some partially drilled as well as unworked discs and flint *mèches de forêt* or drill-bits, whose rounded tips fit neatly within the bead perforations. Modern experiments using replica *mèches de forêt* have demonstrated that two people can make approximately one hundred beads in an hour using a bow-drill.
EAW

7 A microlith from Burry Holms

Burry Holms, Llangennith, Gower, Swansea
Early Mesolithic: about 8,800 BP
Burnt flint
Length 32.1mm
Donated by Mr G. Howells. NMW acc. no. 2000.35H/1197

This flint microlith was discovered during excavation of an early Mesolithic campsite. A series of such microliths would have been mounted into a wooden or bone shaft and used for hunting or fishing. The wood or bone that it was originally hafted into has not survived, but what is remarkable is the fact that microscopic traces of birch resin glue have been found on the microlith. This evidence that the flints were glued into their shafts is rare – organic matter, such as glue, does not normally survive. The microlith was probably burnt while still stuck in place in its shaft; the heat of the fire has turned the glue into a glass-like substance, which adhered to the flint.
EAW

8 An engraved pebble

Rhuddlan, Denbighshire
Early Mesolithic: about 8,700 BP
Micaceous silty sandstone
Length 81.5mm
Donated by Clwyd County Council. NMW acc. no. 96.9H/1.1486

This decorated pebble, one of six found, illustrates creativity on early portable objects. It was discovered at an early Mesolithic campsite along with an assemblage of stone tools and hazelnut shells. The pebble is naturally shaped but has a break at the top; one side has lines incised across its surface forming a crossed motif. The other face, shown here, has two decorated areas. At the top of the pebble are 'V's comprising converging lines infilled with horizontal incised lines. Towards the centre of the pebble are two horizontal lines incised before the vertical lines were infilled between them. All the engraving was done with a stone tool.

The shape resembles a human torso; the break across the neck area occurred after the decoration was applied. There are various interpretations for this object's significance. Is it a figure wearing an apron and a girdle with hanging pendants? Is the break across a human neck, from which a necklace hangs? Could the central 'box' design represent a womb or a stomach?
EAW

9

An antler mattock

Uskmouth, Newport
Later Mesolithic: about 6,200 BP
Red deer antler
Length 229mm
Donated by Mr D. Upton. NMW acc. no. 92.242H

This antler mattock was discovered by chance in 1992 lying on the surface of estuarine clays in the intertidal zone of the Severn Levels in front of Uskmouth Power Station. It is made of part of the beam of a red deer antler with part of one tine surviving. There is a perforation through the antler beam at right angles to this tine. Heavily damaged at both ends, it was designed to be used as a digging tool for searching for food such as cockles.

The mattock was found very close to human footprints of a similar age. These were preserved in the estuarine silts that are exposed at low tide along the Welsh side of the Severn Estuary Levels and can also be seen at Magor Pill and at Goldcliff. At Uskmouth three trails of prints were recorded. Two belong to adult males and are equivalent to modern shoe sizes 8 and 9. The third trail belongs to a child or young person. A number of children's footprints have been found at Goldcliff and Magor Pill. All the footprints – adults' as well as children's – show the splayed toes typical of those who never wear shoes. Studies of the peat have shown that there was salt marsh in the vicinity at the time; the adjacent dry land was dominated by mixed deciduous woodland with pine, lime, elm and hazel. The estuary landscape would have been an open environment of intertidal mudflats and salt-marshes. The footprints give us tangible evidence of later Mesolithic people, while the mattock provides a glimpse of one possible reason for their presence on this soft ground some 6,200 years ago.
EAW

Neolithic

ABOUT 4000 TO 2500 BC

Samuel Hazzeldine Warren excavating at Graig Lwyd in Conwy in 1920.

The Neolithic (New Stone Age) lasted from 4000 to 2500 BC. During these 1,500 years farming, the industrial exploitation of Wales's mineral resources and the large scale clearing of the wild woods – foundations of life in modern Wales – all started. Without farmed produce Wales could not support its three million people. Without the centuries of quarrying and mining Wales would not have much of its heritage and modern identity. Without management of the landscape Wales's countryside would have a very different character. Stone slabs on which wheat and barley were ground to make bread and the bones of domestic sheep illustrate this innovation.

The most obvious remnants of the Neolithic in Wales are megalithic tombs – over one hundred dot the landscape. They are Wales's earliest surviving architecture and have been honey pots for archaeologists. The Museum's collections contain a large quantity of grave goods from these sites (for example pots, stone tools and bone pins) as well as the remains of around a hundred people. The rituals of death that were conducted at these tombs were in stark contrast to our own: the dead were buried together in piles, some were defleshed before being laid to rest, some were revisited and their bones shuffled and others were cremated.

While people had been making tools from Wales's stone for millennia, it is only in the Neolithic that specific stone sources were systematically exploited. The products from these 'axe factories', in Gwynedd and Pembrokeshire, were carried across

Pentre Ifan chambered tomb in Pembrokeshire.

Britain as far as Dorset and Essex. Stone axes, the focus of this trade, are the leitmotif of the Neolithic. The Neolithic also saw the introduction of pottery into Wales – a new medium through which cultural affinity and decorative styles could be expressed. More practically, pottery provided a new method for storing foods, and made some cooking techniques easier.

There has been much debate as to whether people in the Neolithic were 'noble savages' or whether they lived lives that were 'nasty, brutish and short'. The collections shed fresh light on the subject. Hundreds of stone arrowheads have been found in Wales – one was found embedded in the rib of a man buried in a tomb. This discovery has led to other finds, for example, two skulls from Tinkinswood, not far from Cardiff, both fractured by blunt instruments. It seems that the Neolithic was as dangerous a time as any other.

Unlike in later periods, there is little evidence for personal wealth or status in the Neolithic. But, towards its end, individuals began to be buried in single graves, as though to preserve their memory, and the construction of large and enigmatic timber and earth enclosures suggest the presence of powerful leaders. Neolithic people also indulged a fancy for decoration: flint scrapers were carefully polished and mace-heads were produced, sometimes with elaborate carving. People were choosing to make their property distinctive, perhaps marking an increased emphasis on the position of the individual in society.
Steve Burrow

10

The Graig Lwyd axe

Gop Cave, Flintshire
4000–2500 BC
Augite granophyre
Length 305mm; width 95mm; thickness 44mm
Bequeathed by Mr J. H. Morris. NMW acc. no. 47.101/1

The stone axehead is one of the most easily recognizable elements of Neolithic culture; thousands have been found across the British Isles and continental Europe.

Stone blades like this were held in wooden hafts, now long since decayed. Traditionally, it is believed that they were used to clear the woodland around settlements, and it has been proven that trees with a girth of about 900 millimetres can be felled in around thirty minutes. But not all axes were used for this purpose. An axe that chops down a tree can be just as effective at delivering a killing blow, indeed, in an age before swords it is the most obvious candidate for a heavy personal weapon.

Many of these axes were probably made from rocks available locally in riverbeds or in the gravels and clays left behind by glaciers. But a large percentage of Wales's axes are derived from specific outcrops in Pembrokeshire and Gwynedd.

The largest of these so-called axe factories is at Graig Lwyd above Penmaenmawr in Gwynedd. Here there is abundant evidence of Neolithic axe making in the form of mounds of flaked stone, broken axe roughouts and rock outcrops still bearing the scars of early working. For communities living in the adjacent lowlands, it seems that a trip up the mountain to extract rock was a regular activity. The finished axes, often highly polished, also had a role as items for exchange. Graig Lwyd axes have been found across the British Isles, from Cornwall to Yorkshire and from the Isle of Man to Sussex. Presumably they had passed through many hands over many generations before being discarded in these places and, so far from the mountain, they were probably valued as strange and exotic items.
SB

11

A grinding slab

Gwernvale, Crickhowell, Powys
Early Neolithic: 4000-3600 BC
Old Red Sandstone
Length 360mm; width 220mm; thickness 75mm
NMW acc. no. 79.54H/2

The user of this tool would have sat at one end of the large slab, using a smaller stone to grind down hard foods. It is a timeless tool, the forerunner of both the millstone and the household mortar and pestle, and was probably used for grinding wheat and barley. These domesticated plants have their origins in the Middle East and were carried across Europe by early farmers as they spread westwards, arriving in Wales around 4000 BC.

Grinding slabs were a necessary tool for crushing these new hard cereal grains, and the flour that was produced formed the basis for a new food: bread. For the first people to try it, it must have been a great delicacy, produced from a strange new plant that could be grown almost on demand and involving new rituals of preparation. The end result was a food with an unmatched taste; doubtless there was prestige to be had in possessing this innovation.
SB

12 A rib with an arrow wound

Penywyrlod, near Talgarth, Powys
Early Neolithic: about 3650 BC
Human bone
Surviving length 76mm; width of arrow tip 3.6mm
Donated by Mr P. P. Griffiths. NMW acc. no. 74.23H/9.24

The image of Stone Age man evokes different sentiments from different people. For some there is the image of the primitive, constantly locked in an unequal struggle with nature. For others there is the vision of the noble savage, unfettered by the constraints and negativity of civilization. For many years the evidence has leaned towards the latter view, but this bone is part of a growing body of evidence that not everything was peace and harmony at that time. It is part of a human rib found, along with bones from several other people, in a tomb at Penywyrlod. Embedded within it is the tip of an arrow. This wound would not itself have been fatal, but since there is no new bone growth around the flint fragment we know that this person died shortly after they were shot. Most likely it was not the only wound they suffered that day. Is this evidence of a tragic hunting accident, a murder or death in battle?
SB

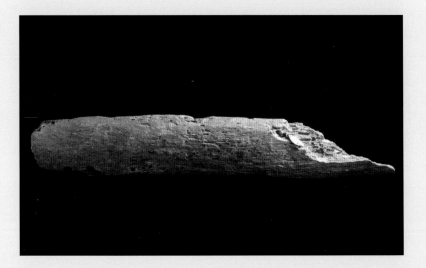

13 Wales's earliest musical instrument?

Penywyrlod, near Talgarth, Powys
Early Neolithic: about 3650 BC
Sheep bone
Length 85mm; diameter 17mm
Donated by Mr P. P. Griffiths. NMW acc. no. 74.23H/6

There are over eleven million sheep in Wales today. This is a leg bone from one of the very first. Sheep are not native to Wales – they were imported around 4000 BC when farming was introduced into the country. The first ones were wiry creatures, more useful for their meat than for their wool. But they had several advantages over wild animals like deer. They were not afraid of people and could be herded, milked and bred: each one was a walking larder. This bone was found in a tomb built by these first farmers, and it has attracted particular attention because of the holes found along its length, which may have been deliberately cut to make a simple whistle. If this is the case, then this is the earliest musical instrument to survive from Wales – but there is uncertainty. The holes are rather crude, suggesting to some that they were made by an animal chewing on the bone to extract marrow, rather than by an early musician. The debate continues.
SB

14 The earliest face from Wales

Penywyrlod, near Talgarth, Powys
Early Neolithic: about 3650 BC
Resin
NMW acc. no. 2006.20H

This image shows a reconstruction of a face from about 3650 BC – the oldest face from Wales. It was found in a stone tomb discovered in 1971, when a farmer began to clear a mound of stone from a field and inadvertently broke into a chamber. The skull was one of the first things to be seen, resting on a layer of jumbled bones, the remains of several people.

The man died aged between twenty-five and thirty – in the prime of life – and the cause of his death is unknown. A slight pitting on his skull's surface suggests that he had suffered from a scalp disorder, but he shows no other signs of ill health.

This is Stone Age man, one of the first farmers. Although he lived almost 6,000 years ago, he looks no different than modern Western man. There is nothing of the primitive about him. He is a stark reminder that without our bought technologies, we ourselves are simply Stone Age people.
SB

15 A decorated stone

Bryn Celli Ddu, Anglesey
Middle Neolithic: about 3000 BC
Grit
Height 1,520mm; width 590mm; thickness 310mm
Lent by the Marquess of Anglesey. NMW acc. no. 29.403

Archaeologists working in the 1920s discovered this stone lying on the ground beneath a burial mound at Bryn Celli Ddu. Sealed beneath it were small pieces of blackthorn and cherry charcoal. These fragments were of little interest at the time, but they were preserved in the national archaeology collections for eighty years until their recent use in a programme of radiocarbon dating of the site. Thanks to these we now know that the stone was laid in place around 3000 BC.

The swirling mass of decoration on the stone made it especially interesting and has provided a source of enduring fascination for subsequent archaeologists. It has been argued that it represents the memory of trance-like states, and this last suggestion seems appropriate since the stone was found beneath a tomb: communing with the spirits of the dead has been a very human theme throughout our history, and many different approaches have been taken to achieve this end.

The mound of the tomb was probably built soon after the stone was set in position, sealing it out of sight for five thousand years. It is possible that it was intended to consecrate the ground for the dead; certainly, the living were not the audience for its carvings once the tomb was built.

Decorated stones have been concealed within similar burial mounds in Brittany and Ireland and carvings in this style are also known from Portugal to Orkney; the stone carver or carvers of Bryn Celli Ddu were part of a cultural tradition that linked them to people across a 2,500-kilometre length of the western Atlantic seaboard.
SB

16 A decorated mace head

Maesmor, near Corwen, Denbighshire
Middle Neolithic: about 3000 BC
Flint
Length 76mm; width 52mm; height 50mm
Lent by National Museums Scotland. NMW acc. no. 82.19H

This mace head is one of the finest examples of Stone Age craftsmanship to have been found in Britain. It is made from a piece of flint, carefully chipped to shape before the surface was ground and smoothed with sand and water. Only one flaw can be found in the design, a minor discrepancy where the first carved facet does not meet the last.

It is assumed that this was a ceremonial piece made around 3000 BC – a symbol of power at a time before gold and jewels. Originally mounted on a haft, it may have been held aloft when the community gathered together, reflecting status on its owner and demonstrating the skill of its maker. In contrast, it was found in humble circumstances, discovered by a labourer while grubbing in a wood on the Maesmor estate around 1840.
SB

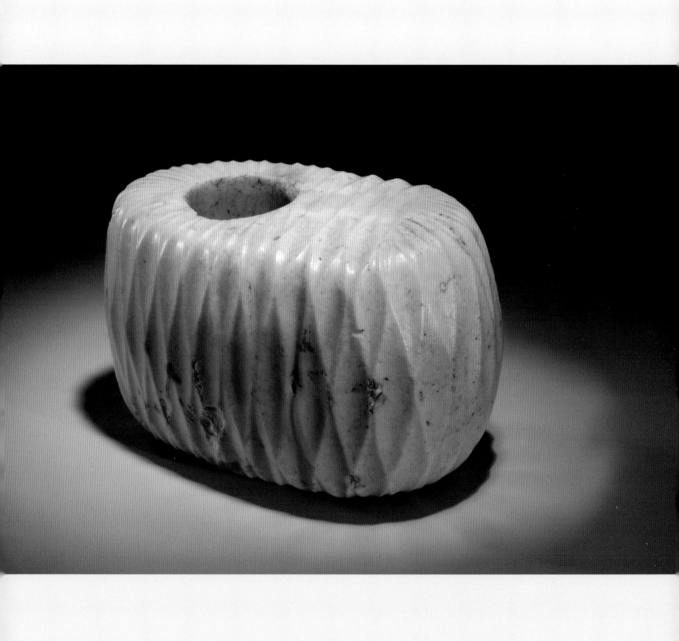

17 An early Neolithic bowl

Tŷ Isaf, near Talgarth, Powys
Neolithic: 4000-3000 BC
Pottery
Height 140mm; diameter 246mm
NMW acc. no. 39.210/1

This bowl was placed in the chamber of a tomb around 3650 BC and was found broken into dozens of pieces by museum archaeologist W. F. Grimes in the 1930s. It was expertly restored in 2006.

Pottery was introduced into Britain and Ireland a little after 4000 BC and was quickly adopted by people in all areas where clay and crushed shell or stone could be obtained easily. The process by which these uninspiring materials were converted into fine polished pottery must have seemed almost magical at first.

Pottery complemented the existing materials used to make bags and bowls – skin, basketry and string. Its fragility set it at a disadvantage in some respects, but it did possess one significant advantage: although bowls made from other materials could be placed over a flame, pottery was much more resilient to heat. Some cooking techniques were therefore much easier once pottery was known.
SB

Bronze Age

ABOUT 2500 TO 800 BC

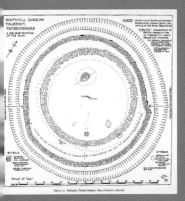

Sir Cyril Fox's reconstruction drawing of a barrow at Talbenny, Pembrokeshire.

The use of metal objects and the spread of metalworking across Britain created powerful social forces and new cultural values. Copper and gold were the first metals. Soon after, bronze, an alloy of copper and tin, replaced copper. Those who lived near and exploited metal ore sources, possessed the magical casting technologies and controlled the movements of prestigious metal objects, increasingly held positions of power. For over 1,500 years these concerns sustained the ranked and status-conscious societies of the Bronze Age.

Initially, Wales was influenced by two metal-working traditions, from Ireland and continental Europe. However, Wales was rich in sources of both copper and gold. Copper mines across north-west and mid-Wales became powerful suppliers, while influential bronze-casting workshops emerged nearby, using tin transported from Cornwall. Among the best preserved mines in Europe, their heyday spanned the six hundred years between 2000 and 1400 BC. Examples include the opencast mine on Copa Hill in Cwmystwyth, Ceredigion and the underground mine complex at the Great Orme near Llandudno.

The archaeology of the Early Bronze Age is dominated by circular burial and ritual monuments. Graves covered with large mounds of earth or stone are known in their many hundreds across both upland and lowland landscapes of Wales. They are often found in cemetery groups, forming recognizable burial and ritual foci. Many have single central burials, later burials being inserted into the mound, as the kin or community members of the founding burials. These monuments connected people with land and the ancestors.

Customs surrounding death and burial can help us to understand the lives of the living. The selection of varied grave goods either represented the individual as in life or symbolized the concerns and identities of the mourning relatives. For example, the fine arrows found in the grave at Breach Farm near Llanblethian in the Vale of Glamorgan attest to a powerful warrior archer. However, the sun design on the accompanying small pot suggests a widely shared belief.

The material cultures of the Bronze Age are outstanding for their diversity and richness: these people were both stylish and colourful. The decorations on pots such as the drinking beaker from Naaboth's Vineyard provide a possible glimpse of early clothing and textile designs. The use of jet, gold, faience and amber marked out the powerful and their ability to acquire exotic goods. Through the technique and elegance of the gold jewellery in the Burton Hoard from Wrexham we can appreciate the art of the Atlantic goldsmith. The increasingly complex weaponry of the time tells us about the role of warriors, both bloody and ceremonial. Few settlements are known, although during the later Bronze Age the timber roundhouse emerged as a new distinctive architectural style. Small farms inhabited by family groups are typical, though defended hilltop enclosures also began to appear in some areas as pressure for good agricultural land grew. Groups of gold torcs and bracelets, bronze tools and weapons were now increasingly and carefully buried as hoards in isolated places away from settlements. These suggest conspicuous acts of giving to deities during powerful community rituals – offering glimpses of an unfamiliar world.

The Bronze Age was a time of expansive and outward-looking connections made between people across Europe long before the invention of money. Here, exchange and long-distance transport were controlled by the select few. The Caergwrle bowl, representing a boat, and the Parc-y-Meirch horse harness are witness to the prestige afforded to seafaring and long-distance journeying during this 'Age of Heroes'.
Adam Gwilt

The remains of a Bronze Age roundhouse excavated at Llanmaes, Vale of Glamorgan, in 2005. The excavation team are marking the post-holes.

18

A sun-disc and mine drain

Banc Tynddol and Copa Hill, Cwmystwyth, Ceredigion
Early Bronze Age: 2500–2000 BC
Gold and timber
Diameter of disc 39mm; surviving drain length 4.7m
Treasure (Treasure Act 1996). NMW acc. no. 2004.61H

The drain being excavated in the laboratory.

A reconstruction drawing of the sun-disc.

This 'sun-disc' is the oldest worked object of gold from Wales. Found in 2002 during exploratory excavations in the vicinity of the Copa Hill mine, it was buried in a grave covered by a stone cairn. The disc was probably attached, like a large button, to the funeral clothing of the deceased. Perhaps this was an early prospector from Ireland, where similar sun-discs and early copper mining evidence are found.

Copper mining began in Wales over 4,000 years ago. Ancient mines have recently been discovered across mid- and north-west Wales, including the opencast mine on Copa Hill. Together, they are among the best studied and best preserved Bronze Age mines in Europe.

Excavation and survey of the Copa Hill mine indicate the miners used fire, stone hammers and antler picks to cut into the rock, chasing veins of ore. Drains, formed from hollowed-out tree trunks, survived in the mine. This example, made from an alder tree trunk, was discovered in 1993. It lay in its original position, where it had once drained water away from a deep mine cutting. Located in a treeless upland landscape, these drains and hammer-stones must have been laboriously carried up the mountain. Remarkably, axe marks survived on the inner surfaces of this drain, indicating that an early bronze flat-axe with a flaring blade was used to shape it.

This mine was probably worked by small groups of seasonal miners each year. During its life of around 300 years the mine produced two to four tons of copper: enough metal to make 5,000–20,000 bronze axes. Long-distance exchanges of metals were being organized at this time, and tin from Cornwall would have been alloyed with the copper to make bronze.
AG

19 A decorated beaker

Naaboth's Vineyard, Llanharry, Rhondda Cynon Taf
Early Bronze Age: 2250-1900 BC
Height 200mm; diameter 163mm
Loan. NMW acc. no. 29.430/1

Changing identities and beliefs among Early Bronze Age people would have been expressed in many ways during their lives. However, it is in death and through their burial monuments that evidence for these beliefs can still be found.

In September 1929, workmen building a new road uncovered a stone-lined grave. It protected the bones of an adult male lying on his right side with his knees drawn up under his chin. Before sealing the grave, mourners had carefully placed this specially made and beautifully decorated beaker beside him. It contained 'slimy stuff' – perhaps the remains of a farewell drink of beer – which was washed out by the workmen who found it.

The time and care taken to create such an intricate design emphasizes the beaker's importance. New research has shown that the pattern was originally filled in with white crushed bone.

Burials of this kind, sometimes accompanied by daggers, arrowheads, tools and beads, but always with a beaker, are found across Europe. They speak of shared beliefs, or perhaps common aspirations, between widespread groups of people.
JD

20 Ceremonial halberds

Tonfannau Granite Quarry, Tywyn, Gwynedd
Early Bronze Age: 2400–2100 BC
Arsenical copper
Lengths: 271mm & 291mm
Donated by Tonfannau Granite Quarries. NMW acc. nos 33.209/1-2

These large blades were once secured by domed rivets onto long wooden poles. Found throughout Europe, but particularly common in Ireland, they are iconic artefacts of the Copper and Early Bronze Ages.

The halberds were found in 1931, while workmen were removing loose stones to open a new gallery at the Tonfannau Granite Quarry. Metallurgical analysis suggests that the arsenical copper from which they are made probably came from the recently investigated Ross Island copper mine in south-western Ireland. These early miners and metalworkers of Ireland played an important role in introducing metals and casting technologies to Britain. However, the stylistic features of these halberds suggest that they were cast in Britain.

Though blunt ended and unwieldy looking they were nevertheless effective at cleaving and smashing skulls, whether animal or human. The power of possessing large metal objects, and of sanctioning life or death, gave these objects ceremonial status.
AG

21

A grave group

Breach Farm, Llanblethian, Vale of Glamorgan
Early Bronze Age: 1950-1750 BC
Ceramic: decorated biconical cup. Bronze: flat axe. Flint: arrowheads,
arrowhead roughouts, knife and scraper. Sandstone: arrowshaft
smoothers. Cremated human bone
Vessel diameter 97mm; axe length 84mm; arrowshaft smoother
lengths 55 & 57mm
Donated by Glamorgan County Council. NMW acc. nos 38.37/1-27, 43

The grave goods with the cremation.

The cup's base, as originally viewed.

This elaborately decorated cup and thirteen finely shaped barbed and tanged arrowheads were carefully gathered by a mourning community in south Wales nearly 4,000 years ago. They accompanied the cremated remains of three people and were buried at the heart of a large circular burial monument, known as a barrow.

This remarkable discovery was made in 1938, during an excavation led by the National Museum archaeologist W. F. Grimes. He was examining one of a cluster of mounded burial monuments in this part of the Vale of Glamorgan, none of which had been scientifically investigated. An impressive circular mound of clay and turf, 25 metres in diameter, was discovered. The outer edge had been defined with a low ring of carefully faced stonework, three courses high. Beneath the centre of the mound was a deep burial pit with a scatter of burnt bone across its base. All the grave goods were placed onto the bone.

The sun-like design on the base of the black cup was meant to be seen as part of the mourning ritual, before and after the cremation. The remains of alternate zones of red and white in-fills have recently been discovered, adding to the impression of meaning invested in its making, use and burial. Found with its decorated base pressed against the west side of the grave pit, we can speculate about possible sun-setting symbolism in the grave.

Arrowheads and bronze axes like these have been found in richly furnished graves across Wessex and north-western France. Three further bronze implements, including a dagger and a chisel, were also found in the grave but disintegrated upon excavation. The range of such finely crafted objects in this prominent grave suggests the power and wider connections of both the living and the dead.
AG

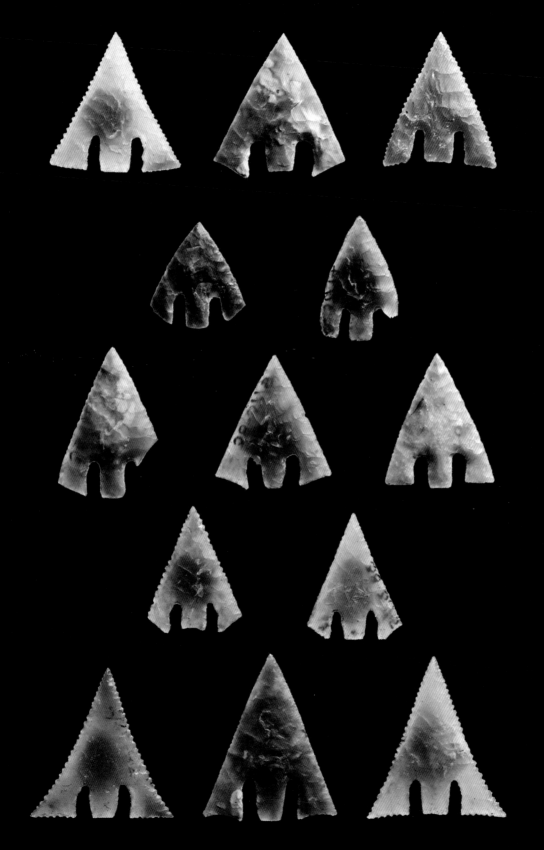

22 A hoard of gold torcs

Cefn Farm, near Llanwrthwl, Powys
Middle Bronze Age: 1300-1150 BC
Gold
Coiled diameters 72-90mm; lengths 870-1175mm
Treasure Trove. NMW acc. nos 54.306/1-4

These delicate coiled torcs, once worn as armlets, occupy a special place in the development of the national collections and the emergence of Wales as a nation. When they were purchased in 1954 it was the first time the National Museum of Wales was able to apply first-claim to treasure trove from Wales, as the Western Mail cutting of the time explains.

The discovery was made around 21 February 1954 when two farm workers were ploughing a field on a hill-slope at Cefn Farm. A large stone sitting upright on its edge needed to be moved. Under this, at some depth, was a smaller stone, which when removed revealed a pair of torcs. Still further down, another stone was found and removed to reveal a second pair of torcs. The finders said that they 'looked like old bed springs' before they washed them in soapy water and realized they were gold!

These torcs illustrate a variety of manufacturing techniques. The two slender examples use a rectangular shaped wire, which has been tightly twisted. Another is formed from a simple circular wire while the largest has a cross-shaped section. The conical and bent-back terminals were carefully soldered onto the long wires. Finally, they were coiled to fit the upper arm.

The report in *The Western Mail*, 1954.

REWARDS TO FINDERS OF WELSH TREASURES

w. Mail 1/10/54

FOUR Bronze Age gold torcs recently found at Llanwrthwl, North Breconshire are now exhibited at the National Museum of Wales, Cardiff. Apart from their great archæological importance they are the first objects declared to be treasure trove found in Wales since, in 1943, the late Professor W. J. Gruffydd, then a Member of Parliament, succeeded in establishing the National Museum's right of pre-emption in respect of Welsh treasure trove. The British Museum previously had the right.

The only other treasure trove in possession of the Museum apart from the famous Dolgelley Chalice and Paten, are two gold nobles from a hoard of 31 found in Borth in 1930, which were bought from the British Museum.

Ex gratia payments have now been made to the finders of the torcs. Mr. J. C. Smith, Talwrn Farm, Llanwrthwl, has been awarded £262 10s., and Mr. J. G. Davies, Stay Little, Newbridge-on-Wye, Llandrindod Wells, £87 10s.

The money was provided by the National Museum of Wales, but payment was made through the British Museum.

Pairs of Bronze Age torcs and bracelets are repeatedly found across western and southern Britain and Ireland. It is possible that these four torcs were paired sets belonging to two related people. These were placed as discrete but associated pairs in the ground, perhaps on their owners' deaths, while the place may have been marked with an upstanding stone. Despite careful archaeological investigation of the find-spot no human burials were found; at this time, people dealt with the dead in ways that left no trace in the ground.
AG

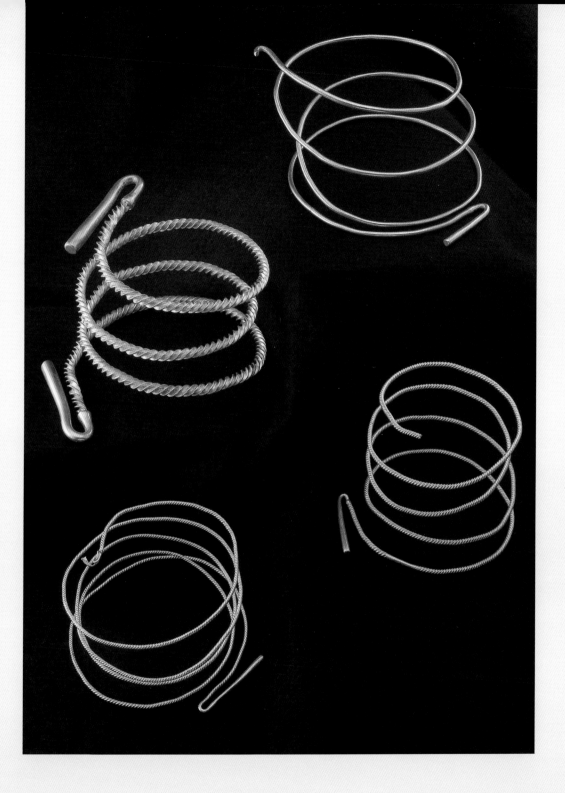

23 The Caergwrle bowl

Near Caergwrle Castle, Flintshire
Middle Bronze Age: about 1200 BC
Shale, gold and tin
Length 177mm; width 110mm; height 75mm
Donated by Sir Foster H. E. Cunliffe, Bart. NMW acc. no. 12.128

An engraving of the bowl published in *Archaeologia* in 1827.

An X-ray image showing the bowl as conserved in 1912.

The Caergwrle bowl is a unique object made out of shale, tin and gold. We believe it represents a Bronze Age boat, with the decoration signifying shields, oars and waves. As well as the gold decoration, there are pairs of oculi at both ends – the 'eyes' of the boat, which probably functioned as a counter charm against misfortune. These can still be seen on many Mediterranean fishing vessels today.

The bowl was found in 1823 by a workman digging a drain in a field below Caergwrle Castle in north-east Wales. It was probably a votive offering, deliberately placed in wet boggy land not far from the river Alyn, an important ancient waterway linking this area to the river Dee and the coast.

Evidence is scarce for the importance of boats and seafaring in prehistoric Britain as only a few partial wrecks survive from the Bronze Age. However it is known that people from Wales had contacts with coastal areas such as south-west England and traded overseas with Ireland, Brittany and beyond. Travelling by sea was essential to forge contacts and acquire exotic materials.

During recent conservation work the old repairs, dating from 1912, were removed and the original construction techniques were examined in detail. We can tell that the gold was attached to the shale using an underlying and unseen layer of tin. For the oars, waves and frame of the boat, gold foil was wrapped around tin and inserted into recesses cut into the shale. The row of shields on gold foil at the top of the boat was attached to a sheet of tin which went around the rim of the bowl. X-rays help to show where the original shale, tin and gold have survived.
MD

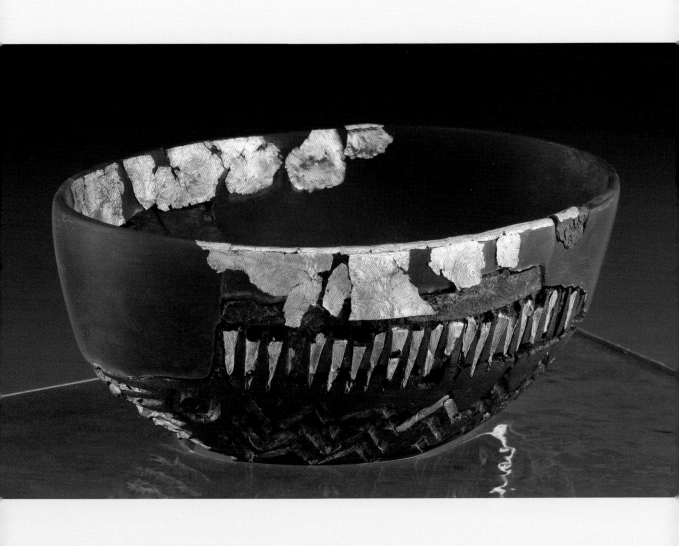

24 The Burton hoard

Burton, Wrexham
Middle Bronze Age: 1300-1150 BC
Gold: torc coiled length 115mm; bracelet coiled length 38mm;
pendant length 26mm; bead diameters 7-11.5mm; ring diameters 13-14mm
Bronze: palstave lengths 150-153mm; chisel length 134mm
Ceramic: vessel base diameter 100mm
Treasure (Treasure Act 1996). NMW acc. nos 2005.68H/1-14

The hoard, photographed when it was found.

This spectacular group of gold jewellery and bronze tools was discovered by three metal-detectorists in 2004. Like most buried gold, when found it gleamed as if new despite being over 3,000 years old.

Immediately after the reporting of the find, National Museum archaeologists were able to investigate the find-spot with the help of the finders. This was undertaken in order to advise H.M. Coroner for north-east Wales, who was responsible for determining whether the hoard was treasure as defined by the Treasure Act 1996. Following the treasure verdict, it was acquired by the Museum in 2005 with grant assistance from the Heritage Lottery Fund, The Art Fund and The Worshipful Company of Goldsmiths.

The gold and bronze objects had originally been carefully placed in a prehistoric pot in a low-lying field near the river Alyn. The torc and bracelet were carefully coiled up to fit inside. The hoard had recently been disturbed and scattered by ploughing. Some distance from known Bronze Age settlements, the spot may have been the place of a ritual ceremony at this waterside location. A number of similar riverside gold discoveries from north-east Wales and Cheshire suggest this was part of a wider regional practice.

Around 1300-1150 BC a new gold-twisting style flourished across Atlantic Europe. Torcs, armlets, bracelets and rings were commonly used across Ireland, Britain, France and Spain. The bracelet, necklace pendant and torc in this hoard illustrate the skill of the early gold-worker. The owner was clearly wealthy – perhaps an influential local leader involved in the long-distance exchanges of metals and prestigious goods.
AG

The GOLDSMITHS' *Company*

ArtFund°

heritage treftadaeth
LOTTERY FUNDED
ARIENNIR GAN Y LOTERI

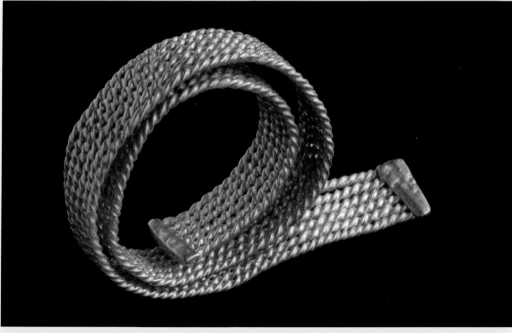

Spearhead and sword chapes

Guilsfield, Powys
Late Bronze Age: 1050-950 BC
Leaded bronze; part of the Guilsfield Hoard
Spearhead length 320mm; chape lengths 302mm & 252mm
Lent by the Earl of Powis. NMW acc. nos 31.62/14, /44 & /50

These weapons were at the cutting edge of technological developments around 1000 BC. By then lead was being added to bronze to improve the flowing properties of the molten metal. This allowed fine spearheads with hollow blades to be cast in elaborate clay moulds. Tongue-shaped sword scabbard fittings, called chapes, were also created with almost paper-thin walls.

In October 1862 120 bronze weapons, tools and items of casting waste were discovered by labourers digging a drain. They were found buried tightly together, as if carefully packed in a wooden box. The hoard, the largest known from Wales, was acquired by the Earl of Powis. It remained as a private collection until 1931 when the majority of the hoard came to the National Museum as a long-term loan.

The name 'Wilburton Complex' was first coined in 1958 by Hubert Savory, then a curator working at the Museum. He used this term to describe the frequent associations of new weapon forms he could see in the Guilsfield hoard and others across southern Britain. More recently the analysis of small metal samples of Wilburton bronzes, including Guilsfield, have identified a very distinctive and consistent alloy signature. The lead component of this may be derived from sources in central Wales.

Why was the hoard buried? Some see metal-workers, collecting and storing bronze for recycling and casting into new objects, pointing to the presence of heat-distorted plate scrap, metal ingots and casting waste. However the inclusion of complete, functioning and high-status objects is curious. Moreover, the violent ramming of fragmentary objects into the sockets of whole objects seems unnecessary. Perhaps it was a gift to gods, with the act of burial itself intended as a show of warrior power and status.
AG

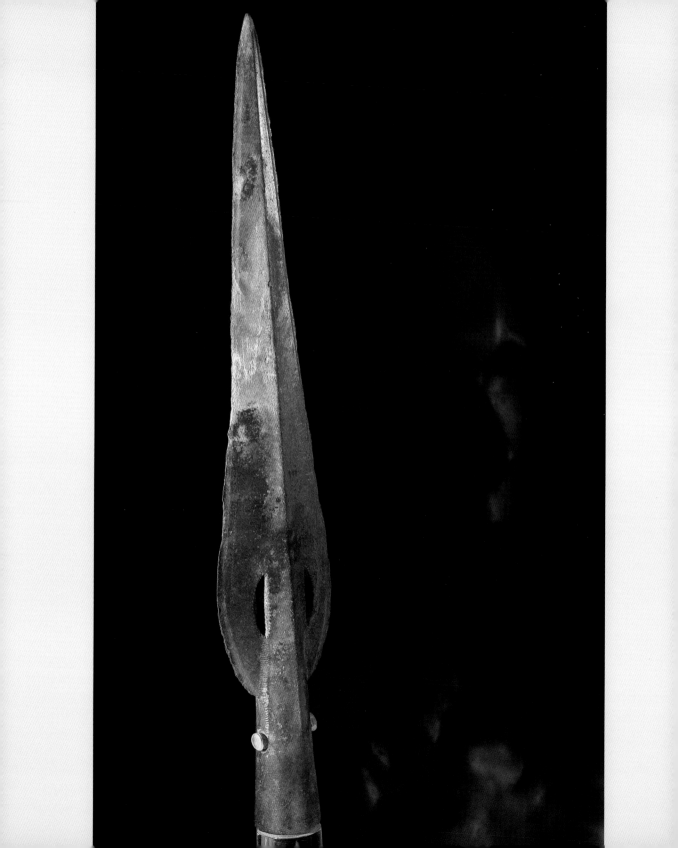

26 The Parc-y-Meirch hoard

Parc-y-Meirch, St George, Conwy
Late Bronze Age: 1150-1000 BC
Bronze
Jangle plates: width 71mm; height 74mm
Jangle ring: diameter 39mm
Donated by the Art Fund and the Dean and Chapter of St Asaph Cathedral;
45 items lent by Hull and East Riding Museum. NMW acc. nos 40.368, 99.33H

A reconstruction drawing of ponies wearing jangles and harness fittings.

This find is the only Late Bronze Age hoard from Britain containing a complete set of harness and wagon fittings. Similar sets have been found in continental Europe and metallurgical analysis suggests that most of the Parc-y-Meirch hoard may have originated from northern France.

Decorating your ponies and wagon with such flamboyant gear was a perfect way of displaying wealth and contacts. Such a sight may have been rare in Wales, and the distant origin of the pieces may have increased their owner's prestige.

The fittings were in use for many years – most parts show signs of heavy wear. Analysis of these wear patterns has led to a new interpretation of how each piece might have been used. Some broken parts were replaced by new imitations. However the worn-out pieces were not discarded or melted down, but kept and looked after.

Perhaps, over time, the fittings took on greater significance as reminders of past journeys to or from faraway lands. Eventually they were gathered together and buried at the foot of crags below Dinorben hillfort, possibly as an offering to the gods. Around this time people were beginning to build houses and defences on top of the hill and it is difficult to imagine that these events were unconnected.

Limestone quarrying at this site began in the nineteenth century and the hoard was discovered by workmen some time before 1868. Today nothing remains of the fort's once formidable defences. Its legacy is preserved in the records and finds kept by earlier generations of archaeologists. By coincidence, the name of land surrounding the site today is Parc-y-Meirch – 'Park of the Horses'.
JD

ArtFund

Iron Age

ABOUT 800 BC TO AD 75

The collapse of long-distance bronze exchanges at the end of the Bronze Age brought about a period of uncertainty and social change. Increasingly, people looked to the agricultural wealth of the land, while competition led to a new-found visibility and definition of settlements in the landscape. Hillforts are the emblematic monumental works of the Iron Age in Wales, where hundreds remain visible. Built and maintained by communities, each of a few hundred people, their ramparts, ditches and entrances were often elaborated over time. At the heart of community life, they could be fairs and religious sites, animal enclosures and grain stores or places of refuge as well as imposing settlements.

Most Iron Age people were self-sufficient family farmers, living in dispersed farm enclosures of roundhouses beyond the fort. Agricultural surpluses increasingly fuelled specialization and the development of longer-distance regional exchanges of items such as pottery, salt, glass and a variety of agricultural products. Early experiments with iron, such as the sword and sickle from Llyn Fawr, were surprisingly infrequent. The new metal was apparently slow to enter widespread use; tools, bladed weapons and ornaments of iron are only commonly found on sites after 300 BC. The Capel Garmon firedog epitomizes the skill of the master blacksmith, probably using iron from nearby sources and smelting sites in Snowdonia.

Celtic or La Tène art emerged in Central Europe during the fifth century BC and spread rapidly across much of Europe. This shared art has frequently been promoted as evidence for the Celts

The crest of the Capel Garmon Firedog.

as a people with similar languages and societies. However, this increasingly seems over-simplistic; the evidence better supports a mosaic of regional societies with diverse and contrasting identities.

Early decorated pieces, such as the Cerrigydrudion crown, share a common continental style. However, distinctive British styles emerged and flourished after 300 BC, adorning portable objects such as weapons, horse-gear, vessels and jewellery. The ever-flowing three-legged motif, the triskele, is repeatedly depicted in Wales. The reflected heads on the shield fittings from Tal-y-llyn bring us face to face with a different world whose meaning and symbolism tantalizingly escape us.

Few people were buried after death: it seems most were exposed to the air or committed to water, leaving little surviving trace. However, the Cerrigydrudion crown may have accompanied a religious leader to the grave. Whether this was an enigmatic and powerful Druid, as recounted by the Classical authors, we might never know. In contrast, many exceptional and prestigious objects were buried at the end of their lives. Isolated places of natural beauty such as mountains, lakes, rivers and bogs were often chosen as places to communicate with the pagan gods. The Llyn Fawr cauldrons, full of symbolism and transformational power, were offered into an upland lake in south Wales. The still waters of Llyn Cerrig Bach, another sacred lake, also received sacrificed weapons, chariots, slave-chains, decorated objects and animals over hundreds of years.

By the eve of the Roman Invasion remarkable social developments had already occurred in Wales: regional tribes and new native elites had emerged. Their concern with personal display is illustrated by decorated horse-pieces, weaponry and personal objects such as collars, bracelets, mirrors and vessels. Thirty years of fierce tribal resistance were waged on the western frontier, before the large Roman Army could control the *Silures*, *Ordovices*, *Demetae* and *Deceangli* tribes of Wales.
Adam Gwilt

27

The Llyn Fawr hoard

Llyn Fawr, Rhigos, Rhondda Cynon Taf
Earliest Iron Age: 800-600 BC
Copper alloy and iron
Cauldrons diameters 550-560mm; socketed axes lengths 88-129mm; sickles
blade lengths 146-199mm; socketed gouges lengths 75-80mm; circular discs
diameters 164-177mm; iron spearhead length 228mm
Donated by Rhondda Urban District Council and Mr G. Stow.
NMW acc. nos 12.11/1-21, 36.624/1-2, 82.86H/1-2

Cauldrons were powerful objects at the centre of social gatherings.
People feasted, re-affirmed political ties and cultivated social
relationships around them. Their symbolic associations with food, fertility
and magical transformations also made them appropriate offerings to the
deities of watery places such as lakes and bogs.

This hoard, with its two cauldrons, tools, weapons, horse-gear and razor
was discovered on the lake-bed of Llyn Fawr in 1911 and 1912 while
workmen were deepening the lake to make a reservoir. This is an isolated
upland setting, with the lake surrounded by steep rocky outcrops in a
cauldron-like formation. Some artefacts, including a second cauldron and
a sword, were only later reported. Buried for over 2,500 years in
waterlogged peat, these artefacts were excellently preserved. It is thought
that they were cast into the lake as offerings, perhaps as a contract with
the gods in return for good harvest and the continued wellbeing of the
community.

The bronze cauldron was a key item of feasting equipment across Atlantic
Europe between 1300 and 600 BC. Designed to impress, hammered
sheets of bronze were painstakingly riveted together. From about 1000 BC
a new and harder material – iron – began to replace bronze. The sword,
the spearhead and one of the sickles are very early experiments in this
new technology. The maker, being familiar with bronze casting,
laboriously hammered the iron into carefully made templates similar to
moulds. The sword and sickle copy recognized earlier bronze forms. More
efficient techniques were soon adopted, as blacksmiths developed
improved iron smithing techniques. 'Llyn Fawr' is the name given to the
beginning of the Iron Age in Britain (800-600 BC), after this hoard.
AG

28 The Cerrigydrudion crown

Tŷ-Tan-y-Foel, Cerrigydrudion, Conwy
Middle Iron Age: 400 BC
Bronze & leather (rawhide)
Maximum original diameter about 265mm
Donated by Mr T. O. Jones. NMW acc. no. 26.116

A lifesize
reconstruction
made by craftsman
Nodge Nolan.

This crown or helmet is the earliest accurately dated piece of Celtic or La Tène Art from Britain. A sample of rawhide (untanned leather) found in direct association with the bronze fragments has recently provided a radiocarbon date, suggesting the crown was made between 405 and 380 BC. The decoration uses motifs taken from Greek art – palmettes and lotus petals – simplifying and linking them to form the new and flowing La Tène Art style. The decoration is similar to patterns seen on other metalwork such as helmets and vessels from France, but this object is British made.

It was discovered in April 1924 while the finder, Mr T. O. Jones, was digging for stone in a small quarry to repair a field wall. The bronze and leather fragments were found inside a small stone-lined chamber. It was probably a grave, although no human bones survived. Originally identified as a hanging bowl and exhibited as such at the Society of Antiquaries of London in 1926, it was then presented to the National Museum of Wales by Mr Jones.

A detailed re-examination in 1982 raised problems with its early interpretation as a hanging bowl. The decoration was entirely absent on upper surfaces, while few parallels could be found. Recently the brim has been shown to be oval and not round in shape. Other examples of headgear from newly discovered Iron Age burials and Roman temples across Britain now support its interpretation as a ceremonial crown.

A full reconstruction of the crown was commissioned by the Museum to help interpret the original object within new archaeological displays. By studying the surviving fragments and decoration from similar early pieces, a complete decorative layout for the crown was recreated by archaeological illustrator Jackie Chadwick (see p.67). Specialist craftsman Nodge Nolan combined this with further detailed observations and measurements to recreate this visually arresting ceremonial head-piece.
AG

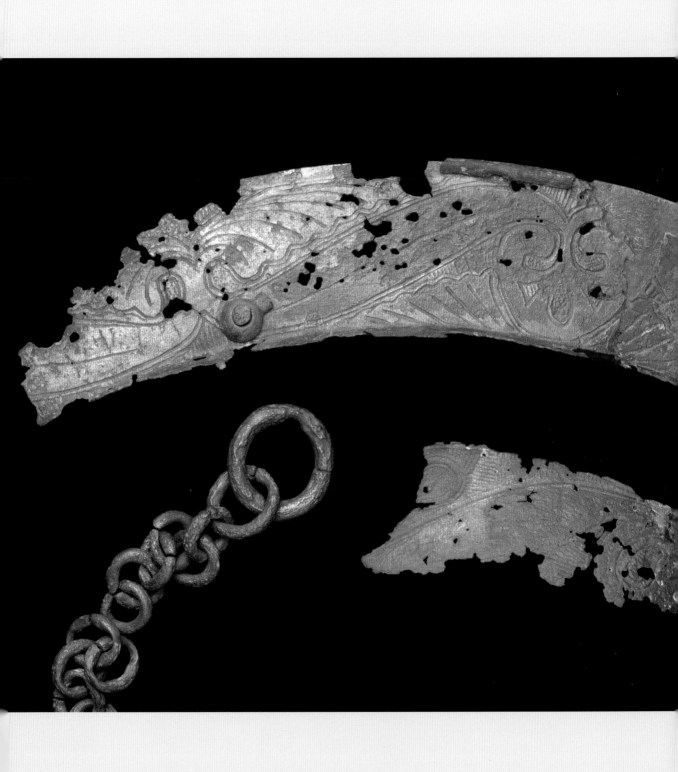

29 A crescentic plaque and bridle-bit

Llyn Cerrig Bach, Anglesey
Late Iron Age: 200 BC-AD 80
Bronze
Crescentic plaque: diameter 183mm; thickness 0.4-0.9mm
Bridle-bit: overall length 297mm; diameter of rings 89-94mm
Donated. NMW acc. nos 44.32/51 & 75

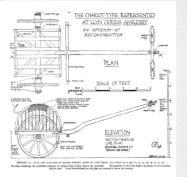

**Sir Cyril Fox's
reconstruction
drawing of a
British chariot.**

On a small island in a lake on Anglesey there was once a religious place of great significance. It was probably approached by a wooden causeway and over a long period of time chariot parts, decorated bronzes, weapons and tools were offered up to the pagan deities.

This decorated crescentic plaque and finely cast horse-bit are two of 170 iron and bronze artefacts retrieved from peat deposits within this former lake. They were discovered in 1942-3 when the runway for RAF Valley was being extended. The peat was being extracted from the bog-filled lake and added to the flattened sand dunes to stabilize the runway make-up. Thanks to the efforts of the resident engineer and his workmen this collection was added to over a number of years and secured for the national collection. This is one of the most important groups of sacrificed metalwork in Europe, finding close parallel with the artefacts from La Tène on Lake Neuchâtel in Switzerland.

The 'Celtic' or La Tène Art decoration on the plaque has occupied the minds of many. Too narrow for a person's neck, some have seen the plaque as originally attached to a shield and others to a chariot. The embossed triskele or three-limbed design is complemented with swirling trumpet recesses, giving the piece a flowing and ever-shifting quality.

Parts of at least ten different chariots and wagons were sacrificed to the lake. This remarkably preserved bridle-bit was one of a pair. The skill involved in its creation can be seen in the way that each new link has been painstakingly moulded and cast onto the previous piece so as to articulate freely. Sir Cyril Fox, then director of the National Museum, was the first to attempt to reconstruct a British chariot in his seminal publication of this metalwork collection in 1946.
AG

Bowls and sword

The Breiddin Hillfort, near Welshpool, Powys
Middle Iron Age: 400-100 BC
Wood
Large bowl diameter 470mm; small bowl diameter 175mm; sword length 401mm
Lent by the Trustees of the Criggion estate. NMW acc. no. 81.78H

Organic materials decay in most soils. Occasionally, in waterlogged places, they are preserved, affording a rare glimpse of the variety of wooden, leather and textile possessions used by ancient societies. The wooden bowls and sword-like object were found in the waterlogged soils of an in-filled water cistern in the interior of an Iron Age hillfort called The Breiddin, which was occupied from 1000 to 50 BC. Large areas of this hillfort were investigated during rescue excavations between 1969 and 1976, in advance of quarrying.The large, carved shallow bowl was possibly used for cream separation or solid food preparation. The deep bowl contained spelt wheat fragments, suggesting it was used for cereal cleaning immediately before burial. The wooden 'sword' possibly only represented a weapon. It may have been deliberately broken and placed into this watery location with votive intent.
AG

31 The Snowdon bowl

Cwm Beudy Mawr, near Crib Goch on Snowdon, Gwynedd
Late Iron Age: AD 50-100
Bronze bowl, decorated bronze and iron handle with red glass inlay
Diameter originally 200mm; width of cat escutcheon 59mm
NMW acc. no. 74.20H

In 1974 two botany students were studying mountain plants on the north-east side of Snowdon when they found this decorated round-bottomed bronze bowl with its enigmatic feline handle. It was spotted partially exposed on the mountain scree – near where it had originally been left 2,000 years earlier. Although only a small part of the bowl survives, the handle is more complete. Here a complex selection of curvilinear shapes has been filled with bright red glass to form a decorative, cat-like face. The rivets attaching the handle to the bowl form the pupils of its eyes. This early Celtic design uses colours and imagery similar to other important, prestigious objects from this period: Iron Age people felt closely connected to nature and the wild fauna and flora of their surroundings. Perhaps the animal-like forms and faces in their art were used to express this relationship.
MD

32

The Tal-y-llyn shield fittings

Tal-y-llyn, Gwynedd
Late Iron Age: AD 50-80
Bronze and brass: part of the Tal-y-llyn hoard
Central boss: width 133mm; midribs: lengths 165 &170mm
Face plaque: length 127mm
Donated by Smithkline Beecham plc. NMW acc. nos 63.419/1, 2, 10

**The triskele design
on one shield boss.**

The fine decoration on these shield fittings captures a world at the cusp of change, when native Iron Age societies were resisting the advances of the Roman army.

For native tribal peoples violence was religiously sanctioned, a battle of spirits and souls as much as a grim physical reality. Now, protective wooden or leather shields were carefully fitted with highly decorated fittings in the 'Celtic' or late La Tène Art style. The repeated three-limbed triskele design may have given wearers spiritual protection and power.

These shield fittings, forming part of the Tal-y-llyn hoard, were chance finds by picnickers in 1963. They were found next to a steep path on the southern slopes of Cader Idris, one of the highest mountains south of Snowdonia. A tightly bundled group of sheet metal artefacts was noticed, half exposed in a cavity beneath a large boulder. When examined, they were found to be the decorated fittings from two shields, with four large decorated ornamental discs and a fragmentary lock plate, possibly from a wooden strong box. It would seem that the hoard had been deliberately concealed, either as an offering to the deities of the lake or for protection at a time of violence and unrest.

The reflected heads on the trapezoidal plaque, one of a pair, invoke both a sense of the ceremonial and the Other-world. Single strands of hair can be picked out in the detail, while the fine bossed decoration is defined by engraving work. Some of the fittings are made of brass, while others are tin-plated. Native metalworkers were making objects in their traditional Iron Age style out of the new metal brass introduced by the Romans. Very similar shaped shield fittings have been found elsewhere in north Wales, which suggests the emergence of a distinctive style of shield during the first century AD.
AG

33   The Capel Garmon firedog

Carreg Coedog Farm, near Llanrwst, Conwy
Late Iron Age: AD 1-100
Wrought iron
Length 1.068m (nose to nose); height 750mm
Lent by Mr C. Wynne-Finch. NMW acc. no. 39.88

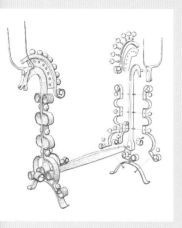

An exploded diagram showing the many elements crafted by the expert blacksmith.

This crested iron firedog, part cow and part horse, is considered a masterpiece of early blacksmithing and one of the finest prehistoric iron objects in Europe. Originally one of a pair, it once defined the hearth at the centre of a chieftain's roundhouse. Seen in flickering firelight, it was an evocative symbol of authority. Similar firedogs have been found as carefully selected grave-goods within rich chiefly burials in southern Britain.

The firedog was discovered in May 1852 by a farm labourer cutting a ditch through a peat-bog at Carreg Coedog. Found on its side, with a large stone placed carefully at either end, it was apparently buried at the bottom of a peat-filled pool. It seems that this mythical beast was laid to rest at the end of its life, and perhaps also at the end of its owner's life.

To make this firedog from iron ore would have required the investment of over three man-years of work. Early iron-working was an extremely intensive process, involving the repeated smelting of ore in small furnaces. This artefact, originally weighing around 38kg, would alone have used 800kg of ore and five tonnes of charcoal. Iron Age smelting and smithing sites have recently been discovered in north-west Wales, so it is likely that the firedog was made using local ores.

In 1991 blacksmith David Petersen was commissioned to make a pair of replicas of the firedog. X-rays of the original by Museum conservators revealed the many components making up the whole piece. The experimental replication showed, beyond all doubt, the enormous skill and craftsmanship of the original blacksmith.

Professor Stuart Piggott said of the Capel Garmon firedog that it 'stands out from all the other British and Continental pieces in its elaboration and rococo flamboyance'.
AG

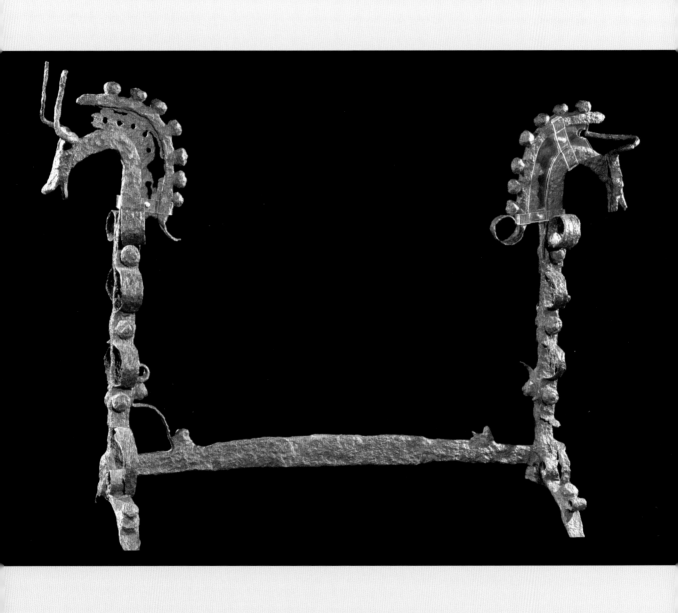

34 A grave group

Boverton, near Llantwit Major, Vale of Glamorgan
Late Iron Age to Early Roman: AD 50-150
Bronze, one with multicoloured enamel insets
Collar diameter 140mm; bracelet diameters 52 & 56mm
Treasure (Treasure Act 1996). NMW acc. nos 2007.19H/1-3

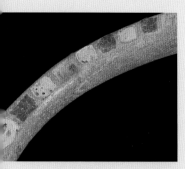

This neck-collar and the half-bracelet were discovered by two metal-detectorists on farm land near Boverton in 2005. A small excavation by Museum archaeologists in association with the finders revealed a second matching bracelet associated with human bone fragments. This collar and bracelet set were worn by a person to the grave.

Bronze neck-collars are found in northern and western Britain. Elaborately decorated in the 'Celtic' or La Tène Art style, they marked the high status of the wearer. This example, with its rectangular enamelled insets, is similar to decorated horse equipment from south Wales, suggesting a distinctive regional tradition.

Radiocarbon dating of the bone suggests that the person was buried during the second century AD. However the collar and bracelets were made a hundred years before this, at a time when the Silures tribe were resisting the advance of the Roman army. The objects were eventually buried as valued heirlooms.
AG

35 The Porth Felen anchor stock

In the sea off the Lleyn Peninsula
2nd or 1st century BC
Lead
Length 1.18m; weight 71.5kg
NMW acc. no. 75.27H

A model of the anchor.

This lead anchor stock was recovered by divers from shallow waters at Porth Felen off the treacherous coast of the Lleyn Peninsula in 1974. The anchor stock would originally have been attached to a wooden shank. It provides valuable evidence of contact with the Mediterranean before the Romans arrived in Britain.

From the viewpoint of the Mediterranean the British Isles were remote and mysterious. The early contacts were restricted to intrepid adventurers, such as the Greek Pytheas. Some 2,300 years ago he set out from Marseille on an astonishing voyage to the fabled lands of Northern Europe. He explored the waters around the British Isles and his account is the earliest description we have of Britain. When Rome began to lay the foundations for an empire in the second century BC, contacts became more regular.

The anchor stock probably came from a relatively small ship, which may have been travelling to Cornwall to trade for tin, or perhaps to Anglesey where copper was mined. But its journey came to an abrupt end in the rough stretch of sea near Aberdaron. The four lumps on one surface of the anchor stock represent knucklebones, which was a game played by sailors. The arrangement here is a special throw, a kind of lucky charm or prayer for success, as it was hit or miss whether the anchor, when thrown overboard, would take hold in the seabed. It obviously didn't bring these sailors much luck.
RJB

Roman

AD 47/78 TO ABOUT 410

**The remains of a
Roman kiln at Holt.**

At its largest, in the second century AD, the Roman Empire covered much of Europe, North Africa and the Near East. Britain was a relatively late addition to the Empire, becoming its most north-western province.

When the Romans invaded Britain in AD 43 it is possible that their plans for conquest did not extend much beyond the south-east of England. However within five years the Roman army was fighting in what is now Wales. The fighting was often bitter and the tribes of Wales resorted to guerrilla warfare. Many people were killed in battle, others in the aftermath. The activities of the Roman army during the conquest phase (AD 74-78) had a huge impact on the peoples of Wales.

Following the conquest a garrison of some 40,000 soldiers was needed to control the tribes in Wales. A network of roads and regularly spaced forts prevented the gathering of hostile forces – a policy of divide and rule. The intensive military occupation of much of Wales lasted for nearly fifty years, or two generations. By the 130s AD most forts no longer held soldiers, suggesting the native population had generally accepted Roman rule. Those forts that were still in use often had a more administrative function.

As a new Roman possession, Britain had to pay its way. Mineral resources were one of Wales's prize assets and the deposits of gold, silver-bearing lead, copper and iron were heavily exploited. These mineral deposits were worked either directly by the Roman state or through private contractors under licence.

The south wall of the Roman town at Caerwent, tribal capital of the Silures.

Britons were not simply left as spectators of the occupation. They responded in different ways to contact with Roman culture. While some, especially in the early days, fought against Roman rule, others enthusiastically embraced Roman values and supported the Roman authorities in the administration of their local tribal area. The Roman occupation of Britain brought about many changes in urbanization, architecture, construction techniques, water supply and sanitation, luxury arts, communications, transport, farming productivity, the market economy, coin use, religion, funerary practices, dress, diet and cooking, social practices such as bathing, literacy, education and record keeping. A distinctive feature of the Roman Empire was the mass production of goods and their transport over long distances. A wide range of pottery, glass and bronze vessels were available.

Wales was part of the Roman Empire for some 350 years. In the early 400s AD the central Roman authorities lost control of Britain. The economic consequences of the chaotic conditions were spectacular. Roman coinage stopped reaching Britain and the structures that provided access to Romanized goods and services collapsed. What did survive in Wales, at least in places, was Christianity and, linked to it, the ability to write Latin. Although the Roman period came to an abrupt end, the legacy of the Romans lives on.
Richard J. Brewer

36

The Clyro 'donkey' mill

Clyro, near Hay-on-Wye, Powys
1st century AD
Stone
Lower stone: height 790mm, maximum diameter 600mm; upper stone: height 660mm, maximum diameter 640mm
Lent by Mr M. Parry and Mr R. Jenkins. NMW acc. nos 2002.18H/1-2

A Roman relief showing an animal-powered mill.

Mills like this have been found only rarely in Britain. The upper stone was found during the digging of a pit for a septic tank near a cottage on the site of the early Roman fort. It was reported to the Portable Antiquities Scheme in 2001 and lent to the Museum for display, and in the following year the complete lower stone also came to light.

This large and heavy flourmill would have been turned by an animal, probably a donkey, rather than people. The grain would have been poured into the top and ground as it descended between the stones, and the flour would then have been collected in a container built around the mill. The flour would have been used for bread, semolina, porridge, pasta and gruel – key staples of the army diet. It was essential that the army was well fed.

The presence of the millstones at this early Roman fort suggests that the site was a supply base during Roman campaigning in mid-Wales. Aerial photography and limited excavation indicate that it was a large fort of some 10 hectares, which could have housed a considerable concentration of troops. The base belongs exclusively to the period of campaigning and was abandoned before the permanent settlement of Wales. It would have taken considerable effort to transport such a heavy item to the fort. In light of this, it is likely that the Roman army anticipated occupying the base for some time, rather than just a single campaigning season. The fort, overlooking the River Wye, was ideally placed either to block hostile raids on west Herefordshire or for troops to move into enemy territory against either the Silures in south-east Wales or the Ordovices in mid-Wales.
RJB

37 The Abergavenny leopard cup

Abergavenny, Monmouthshire
1st century AD
Leaded bronze, silver and amber
Height 115mm
NMW acc. no. 2003.23H

This bronze cup or, more probably, jug is one of the finest Roman vessels to have been found in Wales. It was discovered near Abergavenny in 2002 by a metal-detectorist, who reported the find promptly to the Portable Antiquities Scheme. The cup displays craftsmanship of a high standard and it was almost certainly manufactured in Italy during the first century AD. Very similar cups have been found at Pompeii, which was destroyed during the eruption of Vesuvius in AD 79.

Detailed scientific analysis has revealed that the vessel was cast in a mould using leaded bronze and then finished on a lathe. The handle was made separately using 'lost wax' casting. Some detailing was undertaken on the finished casting: for example the tail and canine teeth, originally cast thicker, were cut away to form finer features. The spots, fifty-seven in total, were scribed out from the body and inlaid with silver. The leopard's eyes, about a millimetre across, were also inlaid possibly with amber.

The leopard appears in Roman mythology as the draught-beast and companion of Bacchus, the god of wine. His worship involved feasting, drinking, music and dancing. The choice of a leopard for the handle of what was probably a wine vessel would, therefore, seem very appropriate. Investigation of the find-spot revealed that the cup had been placed upside down in a small pit containing a cremation. This burial was part of a cemetery beside a Roman road some distance from the mid first- to early second-century fort at Abergavenny. There is also growing evidence for a civilian settlement dating from the second to fourth centuries in the neighbourhood of this cemetery.

Whether the vessel belonged to a Roman officer maintaining the standards of home or a wealthy Briton buying into a new Mediterranean lifestyle is unknown. Whichever, this first-century cup was a costly import and probably belonged to someone of status, who cherished it sufficiently to want it buried with them on their death.
RJB

38 Cremation with grave goods

Brecon Gaer, Powys
Late 1st century AD
Copper alloy, iron and pottery
Diameter of mirror 200mm; diameter of bowl 165mm; height of bowl 125mm
NMW acc. no. 97.7H

During the first and second centuries AD cremation was the most common burial practice throughout the Roman Empire. This cremation burial was found beside a Roman road near the Roman fort of Brecon Gaer. Grave goods deposited with the deceased may reflect status or a concern for future wellbeing in the after-life.

The bowl and lid presumably once held the actual cremated bone, though this is not recorded. They are of a form and fabric used in the Cirencester/Gloucester region and on either side of today's Welsh border during the Flavian period (AD 69-96). The objects buried with the cremated remains are an interesting mix of Roman-style pieces and items of a more native tradition. The largest item is a polished iron mirror with a copper-alloy handle in a native Iron Age 'Celtic' style. To accompany this, but more Roman in style, is a toilet set of tweezers, nail-cleaner and ear-cleaner, all originally attached to a common loop. Also in a native tradition are two copper-alloy D-shaped rings, known as mini-terrets, used to help secure the lynch pins that attached wheels to carts and chariots. It is possible that these may be a symbolic representation of a whole vehicle, as found in some Iron Age graves elsewhere in Britain. The oil lamp is an import from the Continent. This is the most surprising piece, because lamps of any type, let alone elaborate classical examples, are not as common in Britain as elsewhere in the Roman Empire.

The grave could be that of a native inhabitant who had already managed to acquire some of the trappings of Roman culture or that of a retired Roman soldier or his wife, who had done some local 'shopping'.
EMC

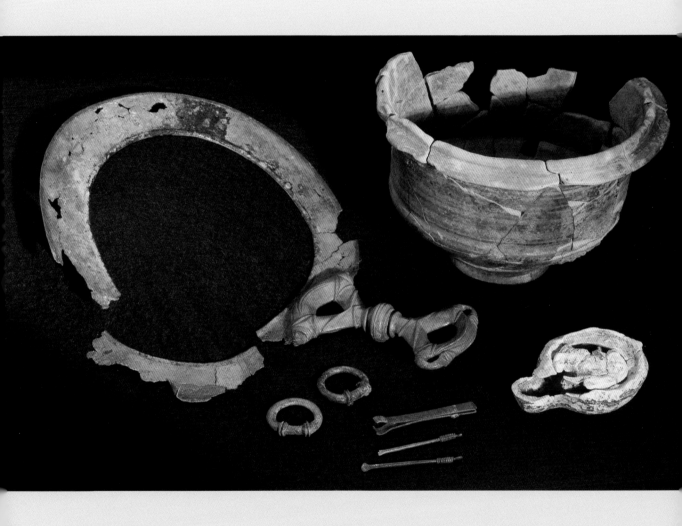

39 A hoard of metalware

Manorbier, Pembrokeshire
Mid-1st to mid-2nd century AD
Copper alloy
Diameter of trulleus 154mm; diameter of strainers 210mm
NMW acc. no. 2005.28H

This group of Roman copper-alloy vessels was found in February 2005 by a metal-detectorist. The group contains five complete objects and fragments of at least three others. The complete objects are a *trulleus* (saucepan) with a decorative openwork plate added to its base, two dippers and two strainers. The fragments include the remains of two shallow flat-bottomed dishes and a cauldron with iron strengthening to the rim.

The combination of dippers and strainers suggests they were used for the preparation and serving of wine, which the Romans drank watered down. Although all are of Roman type, the group appears to come from a native context.

The strainers are of unusual form, having wide rims and no handles. Even more unusual is the openwork decorative plate attached to the base of the otherwise standard first- to second-century *trulleus*. The only other known example with such an attached plate is from Coygan, just a few miles along the coast to the east. The Coygan *trulleus*, found in the nineteenth century, also had a strainer of the same unusual form with it. The occurrence of such comparable material – otherwise virtually unparalleled – on two sites only a short distance apart may be chance, but one cannot help wondering whether it has more significance. Perhaps they hint at either a localized fashion for such items or a particular trading pattern.
EMC

40 A marble building inscription

Caerleon, Newport
Late 1st century AD
Italian marble
1.45m x 1.18m
NMW acc. no. 35.118

The typefaces used to print most books today, including this one, are based on the lettering *scriptura monumentalis* used by the Romans for their stone inscriptions. This inscription is widely regarded as one of the finest Roman inscriptions in Britain and is one of very few to be cut in marble. It must have adorned an important building, possibly the south-west gateway of the fortress near which it was found, reused as a paving stone. Erected in AD 100, it was dedicated by the Second Augustan Legion to the Emperor Trajan (AD 98-117).

The slab seems to have been ordered from Italy with its text ready-cut. The inscription was probably cut in AD 99, but by the time it was set up in AD 100 Trajan had entered his third consulship and the numeral had to be changed from II to III by a less trained hand. Perhaps delivery of the inscription was delayed because ships did not generally sail to Britain during the winter.

The inscription was set out using a grid to determine the letter heights and line spaces. The essential lines for positioning and spacing the letters and their basic strokes were then marked on the stone. Once a signwriter had painted the letters with a broad brush over these lines, a lettercutter chiselled out a v-shaped groove following the painted form. Finally the grooves forming the letters were painted with red lead: specks of pigment survive in some of the grooves. The inscription can be seen at the National Roman Legion Museum in Caerleon.
EMC

IMP·CAES·DIVI·NERVAE·F·
NERVAE·TRAIANO·AVG·
GER·PONTIF·MAXIMO·TRIB·
POTEST   ·   P·   P·
COS·ĪĪĪ
ĪĪ
LEG   AVG

Imp(eratori) Caes(ari) divi [Nervae, f(ilio)]
Nervae Traia[no Aug(usto)]
Ger(manico) pontif(ici) maximo
[trib(unicia)]
Potest(ate) p(atri) p(atriae)
Co(n)s(uli) III
Leg(io) II Aug(usta)

To the Emperor Caesar, son of the deified Nerva,
Nerva Trajan Augustus,
Conqueror of Germany chief priest of the state,
with tribunician power,
Father of his country,
Consul for the third time,
The Second Augustan Legion (dedicates this)

41 A Roman sestertius

Caerwent, Monmouthshire
Trajanic, minted at Rome around AD 112-14
Orichalcum (brass)
Diameter 34mm; weight 23.73g
NMW acc. no. 2007.35H/1.8

A reconstruction of the forum-basilica at Caerwent.
© Cadw, Welsh Assembly Government. Crown copyright.

As archaeological objects, coins provide vital evidence for the dating of their contexts. Of course, a coin can be lost or deposited in the ground many years after it was made, but this example was lost after only a brief period in circulation. It was found in 1993 during excavations by the National Museum, among builders' debris from the construction of the forum-basilica at Caerwent, the Roman regional capital of Venta Silurum.

Unusually for an archaeological find, this coin is perfectly preserved, with a patina that collectors admire. It bears a portrait of Trajan (AD 98-117) that is every bit as good as the more celebrated images of first-century emperors such as Nero (AD 54-68).

Better still, this sestertius is also a commemorative coin of enormous rarity and interest. It celebrates the completion in AD 112 of new harbour and port facilities at Portus. These supplemented the nearby port of Ostia near Rome, at the mouth of the River Tiber, Italy's point of entry for the all-important grain from North Africa.

Trajan's new harbour was hexagonal in shape, 700 metres across and with sides 358 metres in length. The coin's designer has boiled this down to a more intimate scale while still capturing the nature and pretensions of the new port. The near side is opened out, as though the viewer approaches the harbour, and through the entrance three ships can be seen. Quayside bollards and fenders are delineated and at each corner stands a column surmounted by a statue. Most of the buildings lining the harbour are merely sketched in, but the focal point facing the entrance is a prominent building with a tiled roof, clerestory windows and at ground level a colonnaded aisle. Coincidentally, the basilica at Caerwent was just such a building.
EB

42

Gemstones

Caerleon, Newport
1st to 3rd century AD
Semi-precious stones and glass
Lengths 7-18mm; widths 4-15mm
NMW acc. no. 81.79H

An intaglio showing the goddess *Roma*.

In 1979 excavations at the legionary Fortress Baths at Caerleon produced a remarkable collection of eighty-eight engraved, semi-precious gemstones (or intaglios), mostly from the filling of the main drain. The find forms one of the largest collections of gemstones from a single deposit anywhere in the Roman Empire. It represents an accumulation of accidental losses over the two centuries in which the baths were in use (the late 70s to early 230s AD).

These intaglios were originally set in the bezels of finger-rings; a few were found still set in the iron rings that were appropriate to the rank of the ordinary legionary soldier. They served as signets and as charms or talismans. Many depict the deities of fortune and the symbols associated with fortune and prosperity. Not surprisingly for an army camp, military symbols and gods are also well represented, as is Bacchus, the god of wine.

The intaglios are mostly what today we class as semi-precious stones, mainly varieties of quartz. These are comparatively easy to work, but are hard-wearing. Roman gem-cutters did not have powered tools or magnifying aids. Close examination of the engravings shows that the images were formed by the ingenious combination of hollows and straight or slightly curved cuts. These were produced by a spinning abrasive wheel, powered either by a hand-held bow or by a treadle. At the low end of the market, gems were made by simply casting coloured glass paste in a mould.

The intaglios can be seen at the National Roman Legion Museum in Caerleon.
EMC

43

Pottery

Holt, Wrexham
Late 1st to 3rd century AD
Pottery
Height of tallest vessel 200mm
NMW acc. no. 25.1

Iron Age people in much of Wales had little or no tradition of making pottery, so when the Roman army arrived it set up its own kilns. The kilns that supplied the Twentieth Legion based at Chester were established at Holt on the west bank of the River Dee, some 12 kilometres to the south of the fortress. This position is no accident, as it allowed the products to be delivered to Chester by water.

Extensive excavations of the site between 1907 and 1915, conducted by amateur archaeologist Mr T. Arthur Acton, uncovered kilns and related workshops for the manufacture of pottery and tiles. There were also barracks for the workers, probably mainly soldiers, a house for the commandant in charge of the depot and a bath-building. The evidence of the finds suggests that Holt was established towards the end of the first century, probably at the same time as the legionary fortress at Chester began to be rebuilt in stone. The main period of production appears to have been between AD 87 and AD 135, but there is some evidence for continuation, or revival, of activity in the third century up to about AD 250.

Most of the pottery produced was an orangey-red colour, but some fine green-glazed pottery was also made. The potters seem to have produced almost the full range of standard Roman vessel types: jars, flagons, bowls, plates, jugs, cups and beakers. They also produced *mortaria*, the gritted mixing bowls used to grind up food into pastes and sauces.
EMC

44 A Roman will

Trawsfynydd, Gwynedd
AD 75-125
Silver fir
147mm x 99mm x 6mm
Donated by Mr E. Ellerman. NMW acc. no. 2004.60H

Britain's only surviving Roman will, inscribed in Latin on a waxed tablet, was found in the nineteenth century near Trawsfynydd, five kilometres from the Roman fort at Tomen-y-Mur. Originally the will comprised ten or twelve leaves, but this is the only page known to have survived. In 2003, the owner saw a television programme about the writing tablets discovered at the Roman fort of Vindolanda near Hadrian's Wall. He realised that he too possessed a Roman writing tablet and took it to the British Museum for identification. He subsequently donated it to the National Museum.

It was probably normal practice for Roman citizens to make a will in which the heir or heirs would be nominated. It is surprising, therefore, that only a small number of such documents have survived – several from Egypt and this example from Wales.

The tablet is a thin rectangular sheet of wood from a silver fir tree, which was not native to Britain. Although the wax coating on one side is now degraded, it is possible, with careful photography, to discern a ghost of writing in many places. The text is written in 'lower-case' Roman cursive in a style dating to the period AD 75-125. The tablet forms the 'first page' of the will. Its author names an heir to his estate, possibly his wife or daughter, and charges them with responsibility for accepting it within 100 days of becoming aware of their inheritance. The identity of the author and the extent of his estate were presumably detailed on the other tablets, now lost.
RJB

45

The Little Orme hoard

Little Orme, Conwy
Late 3rd to early 4th century AD
Copper alloy
Largest bucket-mount 88 x 104mm
NMW acc. no. 86.24H

This hoard was found by a metal-detectorist, scattered over a fairly level area between the two high points of the Little Orme at Llandudno. The collection comprises five ox-head bucket-mounts, a handle of a razor, the handle of a knife or chisel, two brooches and a horse-harness ring. Sixty-eight coins, all of the usurper Carausius, who established independent rule in Britain and part of Gaul in AD 286 for some ten years, were also recovered.

Three of the bucket-mounts are in the form of simple ox-heads, but the other two are far more elaborate. One consists of an ox-head with a symmetrical scroll to either side, while the other comprises an ox-head with a Celtic-style scroll and a dolphin, commonly portrayed in Roman art, to either side. Both of these mounts bear a loop to hold the handle of a bucket.

Images of bulls and oxen are quite frequent in Romano-Celtic Europe. The bull signifying strength and virility, and cattle representing wealth and status, were revered and admired by Celtic peoples. It is not surprising, therefore, that they often appear as decorations such as these. It is now becoming clear that the Celtic-style art of the late Iron Age did not come to an end with the Roman conquest. Even as late as the end of the third century, objects could display a purely Celtic style, while others combine elements of classical and Celtic influence.
Some of the Little Orme objects were broken in Roman times and they may have been collected for the melting pot to reuse the metal. There was a great deal of Roman activity in the vicinity of the find-spot, mainly associated with the rich copper deposits to be found on the Great Orme.
RJB

46

The Llys Awel hoard

Llys Awel, Conwy
1st to 4th century AD
Copper alloy
Height of Mercury figurine 88mm; heights of seated dogs 54 and 51mm
NMW acc. no. 81.35H

These objects were found by a metal-detectorist in 1979 and 1980 on land close to Pen-y-Corddyn hillfort. Altogether 535 bronze coins were recovered dating from the late first century to the end of the fourth century AD, along with two small bronze seated dogs, another greyhound-type dog, a small figurine of the god Mercury, three votive plaques and a twisted wire bracelet. All the objects and over 200 of the coins were found in a tight cluster over a square metre just to the south of a steep slope. The rest of the coins were found up to fifty metres down the slope, perhaps scattered by ploughing. Significantly, there are a number of springs and watercourses in the immediate vicinity.

The figurine of Mercury is portrayed naked except for a winged hat and a cloak draped over his left shoulder and arm. In his right hand he holds a money bag. Mercury is the best represented divinity in Britain. His classical role is one of a messenger and, more importantly, as patron of merchants, travel, trade and crafts. The figurine is very worn, which might indicate that it had been carried in a pocket or purse as a good luck charm.

Two of the dogs are seated on their haunches with mouths open and tongues protruding, and their stature suggests that they represent powerful hunting or guard dogs. One of the dogs is in several pieces – the tail, the front right leg, the head and upper part of the body and tongue – but whether this was part of a process of deliberate ritual or repairs to a poor casting is uncertain. The role of the dog in both the Celtic and Classical world appears to have been concerned mainly with healing. The presence of these dogs might well indicate a healing shrine or possibly a curative spring, the coins and objects being offered to the gods by believers seeking a cure. Such a shrine could have had pre-Roman origins and it seems to have had a prolonged existence, being patronized until the 390s.
RJB

47 A coffin

Undy, Monmouthshire
3rd to 4th century AD
Bath stone
Length 1.87m
Donated by David Mclean Homes Ltd. NMW acc. no. 96.27H

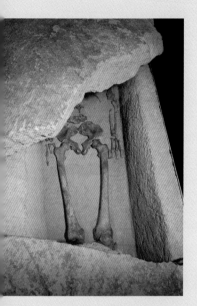

Workmen unearthed this stone coffin in 1996 while digging foundations for new houses. The coffin contained an incomplete skeleton. Anatomical analysis suggests that it is probably that of a woman, who was 1.62 metres (5 feet 4 inches) tall and between twenty-five and thirty-four years old. A radiocarbon date from one of the bones indicates that she died in the latter half of the third or fourth century AD. The stone coffin suggests that she came from a wealthy family – the use of Bath stone, brought in from the other side of the River Severn, would have added to the expense.

Inhumation burial like this had not always been usual in Roman society. Until the late second century AD, cremation was the most common burial practice throughout the Empire. Changing attitudes, notably the spread of beliefs in bodily resurrection, led to a shift in burial practice from cremation to inhumation.
EMC

48

A hoard of 1,424 nummi

Near Bridgend
About AD 310
Copper alloy
Diameters about 27mm
Loan. NMW acc. no. 95.50H

The European Single Currency, known as the Euro, came into being in January 1999. The idea of co-ordinated currencies goes back to Classical times, when from time to time certain Greek cities aligned their coinages. Under the Roman Empire, many former Greek city states continued to issue their own small change within the imperial monetary system, while Egypt retained its own coinage. Following catastrophic debasement and inflation during the third century the emperor Diocletian (AD 284-305) issued a new unified currency in around 294-5, comprising gold, silver and copper-alloy coinages struck to common standards and designs at a network of mints across the Empire.

The Bridgend hoard came to light in 1994 during the construction of a gas pipeline. Buried around AD 310, it provides a marvellous sample of the everyday money of Diocletian's reformed system, coins we know as nummi. By then the system was again showing the strain of inflation and debasement: already twice reduced in weight, a third reduction might have occasioned the concealment of the best hoard of nummi found in Britain for over fifty years.

In AD 300, worried by inflation, Diocletian put out an edict stipulating maximum prices for a series of goods and services. One distinctively British product that appears is a 'hooded cloak'; at 240 nummi this was a luxury item – a duffel coat rather than a 'hoodie', presumably. Like so many prices and incomes policies since, the edict was a failure. The Roman 'single currency' survived in various guises until it too disappeared with the collapse of the Empire itself.
EB

Early Medieval

ABOUT AD 410 TO 1070

The Llan-gors textile, resurrected from waterlogged silts.

Despite prosperity for many during the fourth century, a succession of British-based usurpers culminated in the withdrawal of the Roman army and by AD 410 Britons could no longer rely on Rome for their defence. A new social order developed, with independent regional kingships competing for resources. In Wales the kingdoms fluctuated in size in accordance with the custom of shared inheritance divided between sons, and the ambitions of individual rulers. Although some new rulers might have considered themselves to be heirs of Rome, political power shifted from existing Roman centres to new locations. Records tend to highlight the activities and interests of these powerful and successful members of society, but remarkably little is known about the settlements of its population. However excavations at seats of power such as Dinas Powys near Cardiff and Llan-gors crannog near Brecon have increased our understanding of how the elite lived.

The key to power lay in the control of land and the people who worked it, and rulers rewarded their supporters with gifts. Overseas trading saw a small trickle of imports from western Gaul and the eastern Empire until the early eighth century – the exchange in luxury items and the travels of church leaders and princes maintaining links with the late Antique world. From the 850s trade thrived around the Irish Sea, as shown by the hoards of Viking silver and by museum excavations at Llanbedrgoch on Anglesey.

Palisade planks from Llan-gors crannog.

During the 500s and 600s early missionaries such as Beuno, Cadog, David, Illtud, Samson and Teilo set up monastic communities among their own people in Wales and abroad – Cornwall, Brittany, Galicia and Ireland. From modest beginnings some communities grew into wealthy monastic centres of learning and craftsmanship, and political powerbases.

Inscribed stones are of enormous importance for our understanding of early medieval society in Wales. Many commemorate the dead, and give evidence for the social status and interaction of Insular Celtic with contemporary spoken and written Latin. The use of ogam letters shows that some communities were familiar with Old Irish. As much of the artistic output from early medieval Wales has been lost, particularly when on perishable materials, stone sculpture provides one of the most important sources of evidence for this.

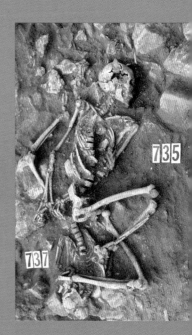

Tenth-century bodies excavated at Llanbedrgoch, Anglesey.

This period was one of profound social, political and economic change, during which the cultural and political identity of Wales emerged. This is epitomized by the adoption during this period of English and Welsh names for the land and its people. After the end of the Roman Empire the word *Wealas* was used by the Franks in Gaul (modern France) and the English in Britain for the earlier inhabitants – both Romans and Britons. It was later applied by the English to describe the British of Wales, in the sense of 'foreigners'. *Cymry*, 'people of the same district', was used by the Britons for themselves. In time, it gave us today's Welsh name for Wales – *Cymru*.
Mark Redknap

49

Latin- and ogam-inscribed stone

Cappel Whyl, Llanwenog, Ceredigion
Late 5th or early 6th century
Medium-grained, dark grey Silurian sandstone
Visible height 1.82m; width 360mm; depth 190mm
Donated by Mrs Davies Evans. NMW acc. no. 50.279

The antiquary Samuel Rush Meyrick (1783-1848) recorded the discovery of this stone below the east wall in the ruins of Cappel Whyl, one of four chapels of ease in Llanwenog parish, destroyed in 1796. In 1808 it was at Llanfechan (Llanvaughan) House in the kitchen garden by the gate. It was moved to Highmead House about 1918, and acquired by the Museum in 1950.

The inscription is in Old Irish, using the ogam alphabet, arranged along the stone edge and Latin. The Latin follows the formula 'X son of Y', with Irish personal names, and reads: *Trenacatus / (h)ic iacit filius / Maglagni* (Trenacatus, here he lies, the son of Maglagnus). The ogam, running vertically up the left angle and part way across the top, reads: *TRENACCATLO*. Maglagni may be an Irish name derived from Maglas, meaning 'prince'. This discovery suggests that the site might have originated as a place of burial in the fifth or sixth centuries AD.
MR

50 A strap-union

Llysworney, Vale of Glamorgan
Mid-6th to mid-7th century
Gilt copper-alloy with blue glass bead
Width 60mm; bead diameter 7mm
NMW acc. no. 2002.76H

Eye-catching metalwork made in Anglo-Saxon England is occasionally found in Wales. Discovered by a metal-detectorist in 2000, this cross-shaped strap-union, used to embellish a horse harness, is one of the finest examples.

The dazzling Anglo-Saxon chip-carved animal ornament, full of fluttering life, shows a highly stylized bird with pointed wing and clawed foot on two of the arms. It is an object with multiple lives. Similar objects derived from elite horse equipment are known from cemeteries in East Anglia. This example lost its original role when it was detached from its leather harness straps and its fastening lugs were filed off. This recycling probably happened in Christian Wales – either through exchange, trade or conquest – where it was converted into a cruciform pendant. The proximity of the find-spot to a royal centre at Llysworney suggests that it became an attractive symbol of elite status for its new owner.
MR

51 A penannular brooch

Newton Moor, Vale of Glamorgan
8th or 9th century
Silver, with partial gilding, gold foil, filigree and blue glass beads
External diameter of hoop 51mm; weight 47.8g
NMW acc. no. 92.4H

Penannular or open-hoop brooches were, alongside pins, popular in Wales as dress or cloak fasteners between the fifth and ninth centuries AD. A development of a Romano-British brooch type, they grew in elaboration to reflect status and changing fashions.

This brooch was discovered in 1991 by a metal-detectorist in a peat deposit close to the River Thaw in the Vale of Glamorgan. The first penannular brooch to be found in Wales that combines the use of silver and gold filigree, it was probably an emblem of rank in keeping with aristocratic practice across Europe during the early medieval period.

There is no evidence for the ritual deposition in Wales of 'aristocratic' jewellery in bogs as votive offerings at this period. The discovery of this isolated find, presumably lost by someone crossing the wet boggy floodplain, has shed new light on a local (British) brooch type previously only represented in copper alloy.
MR

52

Fittings from a portable shrine

Llan-gors Crannog, Powys
8th or early 9th century
Unleaded bronze with enamel and glass
Mount height 55mm
Donated by Llangorse Lake Conservation and Management Co. Ltd.
NMW acc. nos 92.58H/1.1, 1.2

As in Ireland, Scotland and Brittany, the faithful in Wales believed that the powers of saints were present in relics such as bones or pieces of cloth that had touched the tombs of saints. Portable shrines made to house such remains were venerated and used for judicial oath-taking, tribute collection and the greeting of people.

Few such relics from Wales have survived Viking and Anglo-Saxon looting, the Reformation and consequences of later nonconformity. The discovery in 1991 of elements from a small portable house-shaped reliquary shrine during underwater excavations at Llan-gors crannog near Brecon provided the first Welsh evidence for their circulation. Excavations confirmed that the crannog, built between 889 and 893, could be identified as the place known to Anglo-Saxons as Brecenanmere, which was destroyed by a Mercian army in 916. Its identification as a royal llys (court) of the ruling dynasty of the kingdom of Brycheiniog, and an active centre of Welsh power, is supported by other objects recovered during the excavations, including finely embroidered textile and metalwork.

Like related examples, the Llan-gors shrine was small. In form and decoration it is distinctively Irish. The body of the carrying hinge (for a leather strap) is decorated with opaque red and yellow enamel in recessed cells. Two cruciform panels are inlaid with fine blue and white millefiori glass. The damaged circular frame holding a translucent blue glass stud may originally have ended in a beast head, which has been torn off.

The time capsule nature of the crannog, with its short lifespan, provides us with a precisely dated context for this rare discovery.
MR

53

St Gwynhoedl's bell

Llangwnnadl, Gwynedd
9th century
Copper alloy
Overall height 171mm
NMW acc. no. 10.23

Quadrangular hand-bells of iron or copper alloy made by skilled craftsmen were characteristic equipment used in the early churches of Wales, Ireland, Scotland and Brittany. Rung by hand to mark the hours, punctuate the liturgy and ward off evil, many became revered for having acquired miraculous powers. The earliest references in the lives of saints often attribute their manufacture to famous figures such as the sixth-century monk Gildas. His bell was said to have been blessed by Pope Alexander II (1061-73) at Rome, to have twice spoken with human speech and to have raised the dead. Eventually it was given to Cadog, where it was revered and became known as St Cadog's bell. The experience of St Illtud's bell – carried off in an English raid in the time of King Edgar (959-75) – illustrates the fate of many.

St Gwynhoedl's bell, named after a local saint, is one of the largest and finest lost-wax castings in copper alloy from early medieval Wales. According to one tradition, it was found under the hearth at Bryn-y-gloch, Llangwnnadl. It was still being used before 1848 to call children to school inside the church. Stylized beast heads bite the crown of the bell, at the junction of the loop handle and bell body, with open jaws and sharp, bared teeth. Four other copper-alloy handbells survive – St Cystennin's bell from Llangystennin Church in Aberconwy, St Garmon's bell, Llanarmon (possibly twelfth century), St Gwyddelan's bell, Dolwyddelan and St Rhyddlad's bell, Llanrhyddlad.
MR

54 A hoard of silver arm-rings

Red Wharf Bay, Anglesey
First quarter of the 10th century
Silver
Weights 76.8g, 77g, 79.46g, 95.7g, 105.9g. Maximum external diameters 70-79mm
NMW acc. nos 28.215/1-5

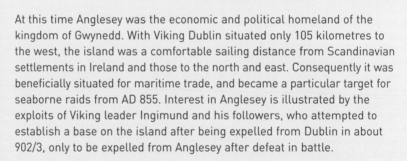

Between about 1887 and 1894 these five remarkable, complete silver arm-rings were discovered at the Tan Dinas quarry near the eastern tip of Red Wharf Bay, probably during the extraction of stone for the Manchester Ship Canal.

The broad bands of silver were hammered from finger-shaped ingots and then punched with different designs. Their decoration is similar to that on arm-rings of late ninth- or early tenth-century date found in Ireland, and it seems likely that they were made there by Viking silversmiths. Made at a time when a bullion economy operated in this part of Britain, they were a form of visible wealth. They are remarkable for their fine condition and completeness – most examples found today are incomplete, having been chopped up to make a desired weight of silver in a transaction.

At this time Anglesey was the economic and political homeland of the kingdom of Gwynedd. With Viking Dublin situated only 105 kilometres to the west, the island was a comfortable sailing distance from Scandinavian settlements in Ireland and those to the north and east. Consequently it was beneficially situated for maritime trade, and became a particular target for seaborne raids from AD 855. Interest in Anglesey is illustrated by the exploits of Viking leader Ingimund and his followers, who attempted to establish a base on the island after being expelled from Dublin in about 902/3, only to be expelled from Anglesey after defeat in battle.

This hoard was deposited within a decade of Ingimund's attempt to colonize Anglesey.

Hoards of this type might have had social as well as economic significance, conferring status on patrons, donors or recipients.
MR

55

The Eiudon cross-shaft

Glan-Sannan-Isaf, Llanfynydd, Carmarthenshire
Cross minus head
Second half of 10th or early 11th century
Medium-grained, reddish grey feldspathic sandstone
Height 2.08m; maximum width 710mm; maximum depth 210mm
Donated by Earl Cawdor. NMW acc. no. 30.47

When Erasmus Saunders recorded this cross-shaft for the antiquary Edward Lhuyd in the late seventeenth century, it stood on a cairn of stones in a field known as Kae'r Maen ('Field of the Stone'), on the east bank of the Afon Sannan. By 1855 it had fallen over, and was taken to the country house known as Golden Grove.

The shaft once supported a cross-head, the two stones being fastened together by a mortise and tenon joint. Its complex ornament links it to free-standing crosses at Carew and Nevern in Pembrokeshire. The personal name Eiudon on one face may be an odd spelling of the male Old Welsh name Iudon. He was probably the donor or commissioner, with the raising of the cross representing an act of piety. This cross could have been set up to mark an early ecclesiastical boundary, the donation of land or its ownership.
MR

56

The Smalls sword guard

The Smalls Reef, Pembrokeshire
First quarter of the 12th century
Brass, with silver wire and black niello (copper sulphide) inlays
Length 98mm
NMW acc. no. 92.4H

About thirteen kilometres due west of the island of Grassholm in the Irish Sea lie hazardous, partially exposed rocks known today as the Smalls. In 1991 a sports diver spotted a bluish object in a gully at a depth of about eleven metres. The object protruded from beneath an iron plate, thought to come from the broken hull of the steam ship Rhiwabon, wrecked there in 1884. The object was declared to the Receiver of Wreck, and identified by curators as a sword guard.

The sides of the guard are engraved with stylized beasts, intertwined with snake-like animals, in a fluid ornamental style known as Urnes. This late Viking style developed from the mid-eleventh century and was adopted in Ireland by artists experimenting with Irish and Scandinavian designs. The flourishing of this style in Ireland saw the creation of exquisite examples of manuscript art and ecclesiastical metalwork, such as the famous Cross of Cong of about 1123. The Urnes-style animal ornament on the sword guard is reminiscent of the earlier Ringerike style, with tight regular bodies, graceful sinuous loops and symmetry. The elaborate workmanship recalls the decoration on the Irish shrines, and it was probably made in Ireland by highly skilled craftsmen working in Hiberno-Viking style for both secular and ecclesiastical patrons about 1100-25.

The guard, separated from the rest of the sword, is unlikely to represent a casual single loss but rather the wrecking of a ship and its cargo of goods and people. The find-spot, along one of the long-distance sea-routes between Ireland and south Wales, is now scheduled under the Protection of Wrecks Act 1973.
MR

Medieval

1070s TO 1530s

**The Great Seal of
Llywelyn ab Iorwerth.**

The Norman invasion of Wales began in the 1070s. For the next 200 years, the Normans and the English led bloody, piecemeal campaigns to bring Wales to heel. Like guerrilla armies today, Welsh princes used hit-and-run tactics and maintained well-armed military households. Castles still dominate parts of the historic landscape of Wales, from early mottes and ringworks to later rings of stone.

In the 1200s the remaining independent rulers of Wales were united first under Llywelyn ab Iorwerth (ruled about 1194-1240) and later under his grandson Llywelyn ap Gruffudd (ruled 1246-82), whose differences with England's Edward I (1239-1307) resulted in ruthless English retaliation. After winning his campaign in 1277 Edward imposed a humiliating treaty on the Welsh. In 1282 the Welsh rebelled, but Llywelyn was killed in a skirmish at Cilmeri near Builth in Powys. Edward I governed his conquered lands as the 'Principality' of Wales; the Welsh responded with grim resignation or limited collaboration.

New towns developed in Wales from the twelfth century as hubs of economic exchange. Some commercial centres like Llan-faes on Anglesey developed under Welsh rulers from the 1100s. Many of today's towns were established under Edward I during programmes of colonization. The sea and rivers were the highways of trade and communications, the range of goods multiplied and imports increased.

The Normans remodelled the Welsh church to conform with the mainstream Christian church on the Continent. They also introduced new monastic orders from France, such as the Benedictines, as agents of colonial authority. The Cistercian Order, an austere 'back-to-basics' form of monasticism founded in the late eleventh century, gained both Welsh and English support. The Cistercians became leading landowners – they owned ten per cent of all land in Wales. They transformed its agriculture, industry and culture.

During the 1300s famine, bad weather and disease caused more disruption than war. In 1349 a deadly disease from Asia, the Black Death, reached Wales. About half the population, which was about 2-300,000 at that time, died in this and following outbreaks.

In 1400 continued hardships provoked a revolt, led by Owain Glyn Dŵr, who wanted to establish a Welsh state and proclaimed himself Prince of Wales. He enlisted the support of powerful English families and formed an alliance with Charles VI of France. The uprising gathered momentum in 1401-2, and by 1403 had become national in scale. Ultimately, however, it failed, leaving destruction and disorder. To this day, no one knows what happened to him.

For over a century Wales was divided between the English Crown and the Marcher Lords until the Acts of Union (1536-43) under Henry VIII, in which the whole of Wales came under English government and laws. Its English-style shire system of thirteen counties lasted until the 1970s, and some of those county names are still used.

Traditionally we think of the political, social and economic turmoil of the Reformation, from the 1530s onwards, as an end to the medieval order and the foundation of modern society. Archaeology sometimes tells a different story. For many people, the break with the past was neither dramatic, nor complete.
Mark Redknap

Owain Glyn Dŵr's motte and bailey at Sycharth, Powys, which was sacked by the English in 1403.
Crown copyright: Royal Commission on the Ancient and Historical Monuments of Wales.

57 The Abergavenny hoard

Abergavenny, Monmouthshire
About 1080-85
Silver pennies
Treasure (Treasure Act 1996). NMW acc. no. 2003.16H

The departure of the Roman army from Britain in about AD 410 led to a considerable period when little or no coinage was used in what is now Wales. From 1066, however, the Normans brought the habit of coinage manufacture and use. They overran Gwent and parts of north and south Wales fairly rapidly, although they struggled to impose themselves elsewhere. This hoard of 199 silver pennies was found in April 2002 in a field near Abergavenny in northern Monmouthshire. The coins were in a cloth bag and had been buried or lost in the mid-1080s. Their discovery was dramatic and unexpected – the first hoard of coins of William the Conqueror (1066-87) recorded from Welsh soil.

There are 130 pennies of Edward the Confessor (1042-66) and 69 of William, making a significant sum of money at the time. Anglo-Saxon and Norman coins name their mints and the moneyers responsible and we see from these a distinctly regional composition, with significant numbers originating from Hereford, Bristol and other towns in the area. In all thirty-five mints are represented – but none is identifiably 'Welsh'. Small issues were, however, struck in William's name at Cardiff, Rhuddlan and perhaps St David's and even Abergavenny itself, though not until after this hoard had been deposited. Under Henry I (1100-35) a mint was established at Pembroke and during the civil war in Stephen's reign (1135-54) coinage was struck at Cardiff and Swansea. Widespread use of coinage in 'Welsh' areas seems to have come later, in the thirteenth century.
EB

58 Enamel plaques from a cross

Probably found in south Wales
About 1200-1210
Copper gilt with champlevé enamel
Central medallion diameter 74mm; terminal widths of T-shaped terminals 60-61mm. Original cross height about 380mm
NMW acc. nos 2004.36H/1-6

During the twelfth century the demand for liturgical objects stimulated the production of enamelled metalwork on the Continent. These enamel plaques and gilded figures from a Romanesque cross resemble those produced in the Limousin region of France, probably in one of the prolific workshops of Limoges, from the end of the twelfth century. These workshops became renowned for a range of products including chrismatories (vessels for consecrated oil used in church rites), reliquary chasses and book covers. Isolated examples of enamelwork from crosses are known from sites across Wales, but are uncommon.

The original form of the metal-covered wooden cross can be reconstructed. The three surviving T-shaped plaques from the cross-arm terminals depict an eagle (for St John the Evangelist), an ox (for St Luke) and a winged man (for St Matthew). The central circular plaque shows a youthful half-length figure of a beardless Christ in Majesty, with arms outstretched. The two mounts in relief depict the Virgin Mary to Christ's left and St John on his right. All are gilded and enamelled, which was popular as it resembled precious stones with magical powers and symbolic associations.

The original cross might have been buried in order to escape the destruction of church furnishings during the Reformation.

The items came to light in 2003 when a collection of objects found by a metal-detectorist were brought to the National Museum for identification. The plaques had lain unrecognized for over a decade among an assortment of other metalwork, much of it Victorian. Unfortunately the significance of the plaques and the need to record their provenance were not recognized at the time of discovery.
MR

59 The 'Levelinus' monument

Near Pentrefoelas, Conwy
Erected 1198-1230
Medium-grained sandstone
Visible height 2.2m
Donated by Col. J. C. Wynne Finch. NMW acc. no. 34.570

This stone once stood in the township of Tir yr Abad (The Abbot's land) near Pentrefoelas – part of an extensive estate granted in 1188 by Llywelyn ab Iorwerth (ruled about 1194-1240) to the Cistercian abbey at Aberconwy nearby. The monument, erected by monks from the abbey, commemorates this generous act.

There have been many attempts since the seventeenth century onwards to solve what has been described as 'the fascinating puzzle' of the inscription. It plays on words in a clever mixture of Welsh and Latin, which explains Llywelyn's Latinized name.

ED.vidh.LN DI.enw alevon[e]
Fortitvdi[n]e:BRAchii:MesuRe
LeveLine pri[n]ceps:Norhv[a]llie

The name Levelin is from 'llew' – lion
And from the might of 'elin' – arm
O Levelinus, Prince of North Wales

Many Welsh rulers endowed Cistercian monasteries. The title 'princeps Nort[h]wallie' clearly linked Llywelyn to a specific territory and his political ambitions. After 1230 he stopped using this title.
MR

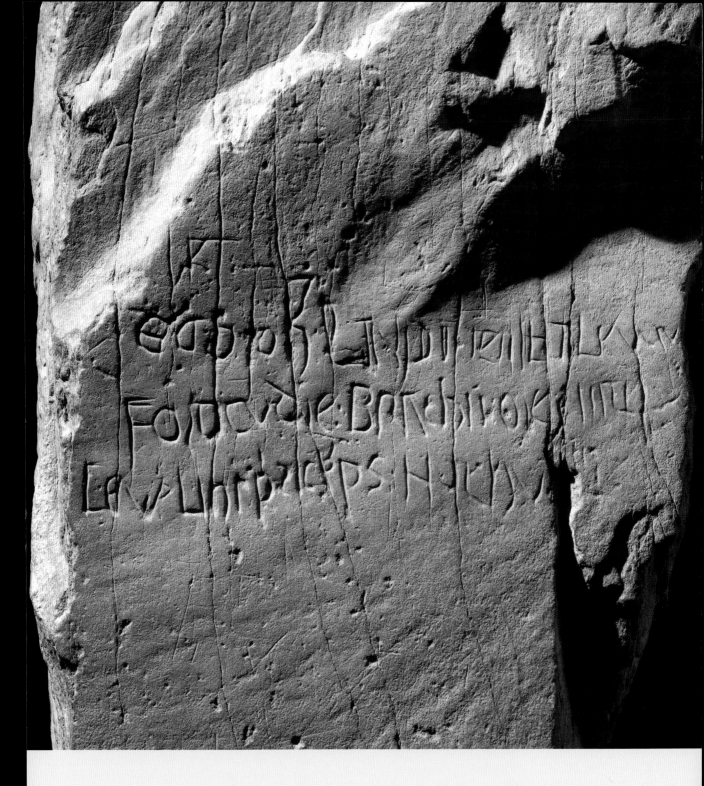

60

A royal head on a corbel

Deganwy Castle, Conwy
Early 13th century
Coarse-grained quartz arenite (sandstone; nose restored)
Height 255mm
Lent by Lord Mostyn. NMW acc. no. 77.11H/10H

This crowned head is a rare likeness of the dynamic Welsh prince
Llywelyn ab Iorwerth (ruled about 1194-1240), who by the time of his
death was undisputed ruler of pura Wallia. It was found in 1965 during
excavations at Deganwy Castle, among rubble thrown over the south
bailey wall, which had been destroyed in 1263. Llywelyn embarked on an
ambitious rebuilding programme after regaining the castle from the
English, and expressed through its decoration his refinement and hopes
to rule a modern state.

The original impact of this head, with its confident expression, is
weakened by the corbel's detachment from its architectural setting and
by the weathering that has removed its colour. The deeply carved features
suggest a growing mastery by sculptors of three-dimensional features,
while the archaic stylization of the hair, the large staring eyes and the
shell-like ears reflect earlier Romanesque styles. While heralding the
emergence of Gothic realism, it remains a statement of wealth and
regional style in north Wales.
MR

**Death of Llywelyn ab
Iorwerth at
Aberconwy Abbey
c.1240.**
© *Corpus Christi
College, Cambridge,
Ms16, f.133.*

61

Silver coins

Llanfaes, Anglesey
13th century
Silver pennies, cut halfpennies and farthings
NMW acc. nos 92.250H, 93.71H, 94.31H, 99.32H

A Rhuddlan penny.

In 1991, metal-detectorist Archie Gillespie started finding medieval coins in a potato-field at Llanfaes, a small village near Beaumaris. He had located the site of the markets and fairs of the thirteenth-century port and commercial capital of the principality of Gwynedd. To date, around one thousand coins have been recorded from this site, as well as several items of jewellery.

Most of the coins are silver pennies of the kings of England from the late twelfth and thirteenth centuries, with small numbers of their Irish and Scottish equivalents. The penny was a valuable coin (a basic wage might be 1-3 pence per day), and for smaller transactions it had to be cut up. Many of the Llanfaes coins have been cut, which is a good sign that this was money in active use rather than hoarded, and supports documentary evidence for the emergence of a monetized economy in the region at this time. But did the Welsh princes themselves issue coinage? The answer may well be yes. There is a series of apparently 'English' coins, produced at Rhuddlan in Denbighshire, in the years around 1200. Normally very rare, many of these have been found at Llanfaes; they appear to have been produced on the orders of the princes of Gwynedd, perhaps using newly mined metal from Halkyn Mountain in Flintshire. Their designs, though, were those of contemporary English pennies ('sterling'), which were accepted virtually everywhere on account of their recognized high quality.

Gwynedd's heyday under Llywelyn ab Iorwerth, known as Llywelyn the Great, was all too brief: wars with Henry III and Edward I of England led to the conquest of all of Wales by the end of the thirteenth century. Llanfaes was dismantled; its buildings were moved to Beaumaris and its inhabitants were resettled at Rhosyr, on the other side of the island, which received its charter as New Borough in April 1303.
EB

62

A chalice and paten

Cwm-Mynach, Dolgellau, Gwynedd
Made about 1230-50
Gilt silver
Chalice height 183mm; cup diameter 159mm; paten diameter 185mm
Lent by Her Majesty the Queen. NMWA acc. no. 10.1

These masterpieces of the medieval goldsmith were discovered on 13 February 1890 by Griffith Griffiths and Ellis Jones while returning from prospecting for manganese on steep boulder-strewn ground on the east side of Cwm-Mynach, above Dolgellau. Griffith first spotted the paten in a hollow under a large stone, and pulled it out. Ellis moved some smaller stones from the hollow and discovered the chalice. After exchanging hands several times they were sold to a dealer at Christie's in 1892 and subsequently acquired by Baron Sir John Schröder. On his death in 1910 they were awarded to the Sovereign after a belated Treasure Trove inquest. They were then loaned by King George V to the National Museum.

This chalice is one of the largest and finest known pieces by English goldsmiths, comparable to survivals from Norway, Sweden and Iceland. Its stem is engraved with stiff-stalked trefoil leafwork and a richly ornamented knop divided into twelve complex lobes. The foot is worked with rows of downward-radiating trefoil leaves and engraved with leafwork. The underside of the foot is inscribed NICOL'VS·ME·FECIT·DE·HERFORDIE ('Nicholas of Hereford made me').

The paten is an accomplished example of thirteenth-century engraving, with foliage and the four evangelist symbols (man for Matthew, lion for Mark, ox for Luke and eagle for John), with MATEVS, IOHNES, MARCVS, LVCAS in scrolls. The centre is finely engraved with Christ in Majesty, surrounded by the inscription +INNOMINE:PATRIS:ET:FILII:ETSPIRITVS:SANCTIAM ('In the name of the Father and of the Son and of the Holy Ghost, Am[en]').

Their beauty, size and the quality of their workmanship give rise to a number of ideas about the circumstances of their burial north-west of Cymer Abbey, but the reasons remain unknown.
MR

63 A medieval glazed jug

Wharton Street, Cardiff
13th century
Lead-glazed earthenware (Ham Green type B)
Overall height 343mm
Donated by Mr B. Mathews. NMW acc. no. 12.149

This wheel-turned jug was made at Ham Green on the river Avon near
Bristol about 1175–1250. Wares made here have been discovered all
along the south coast of Wales and even across the Irish Sea to Dublin.
The jug was 'found in taking up the floor of some back office in Wharton
Street or elsewhere' in the nineteenth century. The unusual frieze shows
a troupe of highly stylized female dancers holding hands around the body
of the pot. A row of stylized face masks or human heads, possibly male
onlookers, encircles the rim.

Dance is an important part of human expression and entertainment,
often in celebration of special events, ceremonies and religious festivals
such as May Day. Correlating medieval artistic interpretations with
contemporary dance practices is not easy, but the scene on this jug
could represent the popular 'round dance' or 'carole' dance, the dancers
being depicted moving in a clockwise direction.
MR

64

A rood figure

Kemeys Inferior, Monmouthshire
Made about 1280-1300, with later repairs
Oak, with gesso, pigments and gilding
Original height about 940mm
NMW acc. no. 32.212

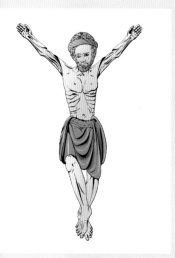

The colours of the Kemeys rood figure reconstructed. The main pigments used at various stages were vermilion red (loin-cloth), red lake (flesh tones), copper green (crown of thorns), indigo, lead white and carbon black with gold leaf (hair and loin-cloth).

By the 1100s Roman Catholicism had become the universal faith in Europe and the crucifix had become a focus of Christian worship. Every medieval church – estimated at 950 in Wales and up to 8,000 in England – once had a rood (the Old English word for cross) set on a beam or screen dividing the nave, where worshippers gathered, and the chancel, which was set aside for clergy. This is the finest of only four fragmentary rood figures from wooden crucifixes to survive from pre-Reformation Britain. It was discovered during repairs to the church at Kemeys Inferior in about 1850, preserved in the blocked up rood-staircase where it had been hidden.

The depictions of Christ reflected changes in theological debate: early ones symbolized Christ's kingship and triumph over death while later ones emphasized his suffering and death. The Kemeys Christ is transitional, wearing a crown of thorns rather than crown of kingship but with a compassionate expression and eyes open – Christ the Saviour, alive.

Its history illustrates the practice of preserving and restoring images during the Reformation. The original left arm was damaged at some point – perhaps following Thomas Cranmer's banishing of idols and images from churches in 1547-48 and the 1550 Act against Superstitious Books and Images. Their removal left a sense of outrage and violation in many communities and some took it upon themselves to hide images rather then see them 'cut in pieces'. The left shoulder was subsequently fitted with a crudely modelled replacement, perhaps during the 1550s during Queen Mary's revival of Catholicism. Eventually the figure was pulled down again, perhaps under Elizabeth I or during the English Civil War, when the rood loft and screen were removed. Its concealment demonstrates the disobedience in Wales to the policy of complete destruction, and continuing devotion to such powerful imagery.
MR

65 The Cwm Nant Col hoard

Cwm Nant Col, Gwynedd
Deposited in the early 16th century
Copper alloy and iron
Aquamanile height 260mm; ewer height 175mm; cauldron diameter 210mm.
Donated by Mr H. J. Wright and Mr I. I. Lewis. NMW acc. nos 19.315,
19.316/1-6, 20.16

A miniature of Pontius pilate washing his hands, from the 13th-century Bonmont Psalter
© Bibliothèque municipale de Besançon.

Most metalwork hoards found in Wales are prehistoric, but this unusual hoard contains a quantity of medieval vessels once used in wealthy households. It was discovered in 1918 by Ifor Idris Lewis, a workman digging for manganese on the south side of the Cwm Nant Col near Llanbedr, at a height of 400 metres. The hoard had been concealed in a space under a large stone on rough ground.

The earliest object is an aquamanile, used to pour water for ritual hand washing at mealtimes or during Mass. They could take the form of animals, birds or equestrian and mythical figures; this one has the form of a stag in an energized stance, whose antlers have been broken off above the first tine. The handle terminates in a dragon-like head that grips the stag's neck. A strikingly similar example from Telemark in Norway, now in the Oslo University Museum, is thought to be of Lower Saxon manufacture and dated on stylistic grounds to the first half of the thirteenth century; the Cwm Nant Col stag may be of similar date and provenance. The ewer, also for pouring water, is similar to one from Strata Florida Abbey in Ceredigion.

The diverse range of objects, including a bag-shaped cauldron, two skillets, a handled tray, fragments of an iron firedog and an axe head, their dates and worn states all suggest that they might have been gathered as scrap metal by a travelling tinker in the first half of the sixteenth century – beyond the main network of scrap collection that may have operated in towns.

The objects were presented to the Museum in 1919 and 1920, except for the missing handle of the ewer, which was donated by the finder's daughter in 1964.
MR

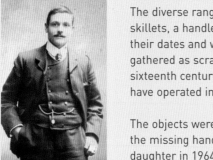

Ifor Idris Lewis, c. 1900.

66 An ivory diptych

Llandaff, Cardiff
About 1340-1360
Elephant ivory
Right leaf height 108mm; width 71mm
NMW acc. no. 01.335

Medieval diptychs and triptychs – two- and three-panel images – were intended to engage medieval viewers in meditation on Christ's life and suffering and to intensify the devotional experience. During the thirteenth and fourteenth centuries Paris dominated the market for the manufacture of such devotional objects from ivory, although they were also made in England, Germany and Italy. Many have lost their original bright colour schemes.

The right-hand leaf depicting the crucifixion was found 'in three pieces' by Mr Henry Bird of Cardiff during the demolition of 'the old well-house' at Llandaff in May 1836. After passing through several hands it was purchased in 1901 by the Cardiff Museum from the estate of John Storrie, who was curator from 1878 to 1893. Christ is flanked by the Virgin Mary and St John the Evangelist as a young man holding a book and turned away from the cross, beneath an architectural canopy. This is composed of three Gothic trefoiled arches, each surmounted by a triangular gable with crockets and finial.

The style of the figures and the details of the canopy and border match those of a left-hand leaf identified in the collections of National Museums Liverpool, showing the Virgin and Child flanked by Saints Peter (bearing keys) and Paul (with sword). The panels also share dimensions and other features that confirm they once belonged together, and they were reunited in 2009, in an exceptional event. Today the Llandaff leaf is displayed with a copy of its partner.

The Liverpool leaf was acquired in 1953 from the estate of Mr Philip Nelson, who purchased it for £5 10s 0d from a dealer in Bath in 1934. Were both leaves found at Llandaff in 1836, to end up in different hands? Were they separated in the sixteenth or seventeenth centuries?
MR

67

The Oxwich brooch

Oxwich Castle, Gower
Gold with rubies and chalcedony cameos
About 1320-1340
External frame diameter 40mm; weight 14.75g
NMW acc. no. 76.39H

This remarkable annular brooch was found in 1968 during the clearance of spoil from a vaulted chamber beneath the hall of the great house at Oxwich Castle (built between 1559 and 1580).

The brooch is set with rubies and cameos cut from chalcedony. These show a man's head in profile with a coif, a form of head-dress fashionable in the mid-thirteenth century. Some constructional techniques, such as the riveting of the collets to the oval hoop bases, are paralleled by jewellery from the Colmar Treasure (deposited in 1349) and point to the product of Parisian goldsmiths working about 1320-40. The cameos are considered to be earlier, from about 1250.

The brooch has been associated by some with the dispersal of royal treasure following the capture in 1326 of King Edward II (1307-27) near Neath. Some royal effects were dispersed following their transfer to Swansea Castle. For ten years commissions of enquiry investigated the loss. Robert de Penres (Penrhys), who then held Oxwich Castle, came under suspicion but later cleared himself.
MR

68

Mount with the arms of Glyn Dŵr

Harlech Castle, Gwynedd
About 1400
Copper alloy with green enamel and gilding
Roundel diameter 40mm; external diameter 74mm
Loan. NMW acc. no. 25.483

This armorial mount, once riveted to leather, may come from a sword belt or a martingale and is one of the few tangible links with Owain Glyn Dŵr. It was found in 1923 during clearance work by the then Ministry of Works of the middle ward of Harlech Castle. The quartered shield of arms, executed in champlevé enamel in gold and black (from copper and iron colouring agents), bears lions rampant, corresponding to those adopted by Owain Glyn Dŵr as prince of Wales, the title proclaimed at Glyndyfrdwy on 16 September 1400.

In 1404 Glyn Dŵr captured Harlech Castle, which he held until it was recaptured after a long siege led by Prince Harry of Monmouth, later Henry V, in 1408/9. The fine workmanship and heraldry places this mount in an elite context. It may be from personal equipment belonging to Glyn Dŵr or one of his retinue. The same arms appear on his Great Seal and privy seal, now in the Bibliothèque nationale de France in Paris.
MR

The Great Seal of Owain Glyn Dŵr, used 1404-6.

69 The seal-die of the chancery of Monmouth

River Wye, Monmouthshire
In use by 1477
Copper alloy
Diameter 66mm
NMW acc. no. 31.78/4.1

This fifteenth-century seal-die was still authenticating documents in 1622 as the Chancery and Exchequer Seal for Monmouth. It was discovered in the River Wye 'by a poor man' in about 1850, and for some time it was used as the weight of a clock pendulum. It is the upper part of the seal-die and retains one of the four lugs by which it would have been aligned with its (now lost) lower counter-seal in a seal-press.

The seal shows king Edward IV (ruled AD 1461-83) on a war-horse or 'destrier'; his shield and horse caparison show the coats of arms of the Duchy of Lancaster, of which Monmouth then formed part. The legend reads in gothic Black Letter script: *S : Edwardi : dei : gra : reg : Angl.: t : Francie : cancellerie : sue : de : Monemouth* ('The seal of Edward, by the Grace of God, King of England and France, in his chancery of Monmouth'). Edward IV was not only king but also Duke of Lancaster.
MR

Edward IV, with Sir William Herbert and his wife Anne Devereux kneeling at his feet.
© British Library Board, Royal Ms 18, DII, f.6.

70

The Raglan ring

Raglan, Monmouthshire
About 1440-50
Gold
Hoop diameter 25mm; weight 47.97g
Treasure (Treasure Act 1996). NMW acc. no. 2000.22H

The Raglan ring is one of the heaviest and most skilfully engraved medieval signet rings to have been discovered in Britain in recent years. Found by a metal-detectorist in 1998, it was declared treasure in the following year under the Treasure Act 1996.

It is engraved with a lion passant on a bed of flowers and the legend 'feythfoull to yow' in Black Letter minuscule lettering. The initials W and A that flank the lion are probably initials for two forenames. Each shoulder is exuberantly engraved with three stylized, pointed flowers on stems with leaves. Such flowerwork is characteristic of some English jewellery of the fifteenth century, such as that on the gold episcopal ring of John Stanbury, bishop of Hereford (1452-74).

The Raglan ring belonged to a powerful, high-ranking noble but it is difficult to identify exactly who that was. Circumstantial evidence – its discovery 670 metres south of Raglan Castle, the date and the initials – suggest William Herbert, first earl of Pembroke, as a compelling candidate. He married Anne Devereux in 1449, and the motto could be regarded as an expression of his fidelity toward his wife, making the motto a private one while echoing fidelity to the Crown and reflecting royal office. Herbert was a close friend of the new king, Edward IV, one of two men referred to as the 'chosen and faithful'. The most prominent Yorkist supporter in Wales, he was created earl of Pembroke in 1468 as a reward for his capture of Harlech Castle, the last Lancastrian stronghold. He lavished his great wealth on continuing his father's building programme on Raglan Castle, but his life was short. He was executed at Northampton by Richard Neville, earl of Warwick, following defeat at the battle of Edgcote in 1469.
MR

Reference

Further reading

Arnold, Christopher J. and Davies, Jeffrey L., *Roman and Early Medieval Wales*, Sutton Publishing, 2000.

Barton, Nick, *Ice Age Britain*, English Heritage and B.T. Batsford, 2005.

Burrow, Steve, *The Tomb Builders in Wales 4000–3000 BC*, National Museum Wales Books, 2006.

Buttler, Caroline and Davis, Mary, *Things Fall Apart: museum conservation in practice*, National Museum Wales, 2006.

Davies, John, *A History of Wales*, Penguin, 1990.

Davies, John, *The Making of Wales*, Cadw/History Press, 2009.

Davies, Rees R., *The Age of Conquest: Wales, 1063-1415* (revised edn), Oxford University Press, 2000.

Davies, Wendy, *Patterns of Power in Early Wales*, Oxford University Press, 1990.

Davies, Wendy, *Wales in the Early Middle Ages*, Leicester University Press, 1982.

Edwards, Nancy, *A Corpus of Early Medieval Inscribed Stones and Stone Sculpture in Wales, Vol II, South-west Wales*, University of Wales Press, 2007.

Eogan, George, *The Accomplished Art. Gold and gold-working in Britain and Ireland during the Bronze Age*, Oxbow Books, 1994.

Fox, Cyril, *Life and Death in the Bronze*

Age. An archaeologist's field-work, Routledge and Kegan Paul, 1959.

Knight, Jeremy K., Caerleon Roman Fortress, Cadw, 1994.

Lynch, Frances E. B., Aldhouse-Green, Stephen and Davies, Jeffrey, L., Prehistoric Wales, Sutton Publishing, 2000.

Macdonald, Philip, Llyn Cerrig Bach. A Study of the Copper Alloy Artefacts from the Insular La Tène Assemblage, University of Wales Press, 2007.

Manning, William H., Roman Wales. A pocket guide, University of Wales Press, 2001.

Mithen, Steven, After the Ice: a global human history, 20,000-5000 BC, Weidenfeld & Nicolson, 2005.

Morgan, Prys (ed.), The Tempus history of Wales: 25,000 BC-AD 2000, Tempus, 2001.

Redknap, Mark, The Christian Celts. Treasures of late Celtic Wales, National Museum Wales Books, 1991.

Redknap, Mark, Vikings in Wales. An archaeological quest, National Museum Wales Books, 2002.

Redknap, Mark and Lewis, John M., A Corpus of Early Medieval Inscribed Stones and Stone Sculpture in Wales, Vol I, South-east Wales and the Welsh Marches, University of Wales Press, 2007.

Savory, Hubert Newman, Guide Catalogue of the Iron Age Collections, National Museum Wales Books, 1976.

Savory, Hubert Newman, Guide Catalogue of the Bronze Age Collections, National Museum Wales Books, 1980.

Stead, Ian M., Celtic Art, British Museum Press, 2003.

Wakelin, Peter and Griffiths, R. A. (eds), Hidden Histories. Discovering the heritage of Wales, RCAHMW, 2008.

Williams, David Henry, Catalogue of Seals in the National Museum of Wales Vol. 1. Seal Dies, Welsh Seals, Papal Bullae, National Museum Wales Books, 1993.

Williams, Glanmor, Recovery, Reorientation and Reformation: Wales, c.1415-1642, Oxford University Press, 1987.

Cadw's four volumes of A guide to ancient and historic Wales (Dyfed by Sian E. Rees, Glamorgan and Gwent by Elisabeth Whittle, Clwyd and Powys by Helen Burnham and Sian E. Rees and Gwynedd by Frances E. B. Lynch) provide a valuable regional introduction to ancient and medieval sites.

Also, Cadw's expanding series of guides to sites in State care are well-illustrated and full of detail.

The Royal Commission on the Ancient and Historical Monuments of Wales has published inventories and a wide range of other publications that provide authoritative information and interpretations for most periods.

Glossary

Aquamanile   a vessel used to pour water for washing hands. From the Latin *aqua* meaning 'water' and *manus* meaning 'hand'.

BP   the abbreviation for Before Present, commonly used in Palaeolithic and Mesolithic archaeology.

Bailey   a castle courtyard enclosed by defences.

Bezel   a metal setting on jewellery for a gem or semi-precious stone.

Blade (stone)   a flake at least as twice as long as it is wide, struck from a core. It usually has parallel scars running its length.

Cameo   precious or semi-precious stone carved in relief, usually so that different layers contrast in colour.

Chalice   a cup or goblet used to hold consecrated wine for the Eucharist in the celebration of the Mass.

Champlevé   the technique in which shallow troughs or cells are cut into a metal surface, to be filled with enamel.

Cheddar point   a trapezoidal-backed blade typical of the Late Upper Palaeolithic period.

Chapel of ease   a chapel offering comfort to those living a long way from the parish church, often serving dispersed communities.

Chasse   a portable house- or church-shaped shrine.

Clerestory   the architectural term for the wall of a nave that rises above the side aisles and has a range of windows.

Collet   a secure metal setting for a stone or cameo, often resembling a rim or collar.

Corbel   a stone projection from a wall, supporting stonework, beams or rafters.

Core   the remains of the flint or stone from which flakes or blades have been removed.

Debasement   lowering the intrinsic value of a metal by reducing the quantity of gold, silver or copper it contains.

Dipper   a vessel used to ladle liquid out of a large container.

Diptych   a pair of hinged panels, usually painted or carved. A triptych has three panels or leaves.

Faience   Originally used to describe tin-glazed earthenware from Faenza in Italy, it was later applied to ancient glazed siliceous wares made in a different way.

Flavian   belonging to the period of the Roman Flavian dynasty, that is, the reigns of Vespasian (69-79), Titus (79-81) and Domitian (81-96).

Forum-basilica   the Latin names for market place (*forum*) and town hall (*basilica*), combined into a single architectural unit.

Glacial   the cold period (Ice Age) when large areas of land are covered by ice sheets, and glaciers form in mountain valleys.

Hafted   mounted onto a wood or bone fitting to create a handle for an axe or tool, or a shaft for an arrow or harpoon.

Interglacial	the warm periods, as we live in today, when the ice caps retreat to the Poles and sea-levels rise.
Interstadial	short periods of warmer temperatures and improved climate during a glacial cold period.
Lug	a perforated projection for suspending or fastening an object.
Martingale	a strap-junction on a horse harness designed to prevent the animal rearing its head.
Maxilla	the Latin name for the upper jaw, the fused bones forming nose, cheek and upper palate.
Mèche de forêt	a drill bit distinctive to the early Mesolithic period.
Moneyer	a person responsible to the Crown for the production and quality of new coinage.
Neanderthals	Homo neanderthalensis, now extinct hominin who shared a common ancestor with modern humans but who evolved and thrived between 250,000 BP and 30,000 BP, after which time they became extinct.
Niello	a black decorative substance of powdered silver, lead or copper and sulphur, fused to a metal surface.
Ogam	the early medieval alphabet developed in Ireland, made up of groups of incised lines set at different angles against or across a base-line (usually vertical on stones).
Paten	a circular dish for holding the Sacrament, and cover for the chalice.
Patina	the chemical change to the outer surface of stone or metal, usually affecting its colour.
Pre-emption	the right of first refusal to acquire.
Reliquary	a container for relics, either the physical remains of saints or objects associated with saints or other religious figures.
Retouch	the fine flake removals from the edge of a stone tool produced while shaping it for a specific purpose.
Ringerike	Scandinavian art style that flourished from the late tenth to eleventh centuries, named after runestones with animal and plant motifs in the Ringerike district of Norway.
Romanesque	an energetic artistic style that combined influences from Byzantium and western Europe into a coherent style.
Seal-die	a matrix engraved with the owner's insignia for impressing wax to seal and authenticate correspondence.
Sestertius	a Roman unit of account and name of a large brass coin.
Stratigraphy	the study of the formation, composition and layering of deposits.
Terret	the metal loop on a horse harness that guides the reins.
Urnes	the last phase of Scandinavian animal art during the second half of the eleventh and twelfth centuries, named after the decoration on a wooden church at Urnes in Norway.

Notes on contributors

Edward Besly
Curator of Numismatics. His work covers any and all aspects of coins, medals and tokens, naturally with particular emphasis on Wales.

Richard Brewer
Research Keeper of Roman Archaeology. His main areas of research are the Romano-British town of Caerwent (*Venta Silurum*) and material culture of this period.

Steve Burrow
Curator of Early Prehistory. Author of *Catalogue of the Mesolithic and Neolithic Collections in the National Museums & Galleries of Wales* (2003).

Evan Chapman
Curatorial Officer in the Archaeology & Numismatics Department. Author of *A Catalogue of Roman Military Equipment in the National Museum of Wales* (2005).

Mary Davis
Conservator in the Archaeology & Numismatics Department. Her work is predominantly on the conservation and scientific analysis of prehistoric artefacts, including recent research on the Caergwrle Bowl

Jody Deacon
Curatorial Assistant (Prehistory) in the Archaeology & Numismatics Department.

Adam Gwilt
Curator of Bronze and Iron Age Archaeology. Co-director of the research excavation and survey project at Llanmaes, Vale of Glamorgan; also researching a range of recently discovered metalwork and treasure finds from Wales.

Mark Redknap
Acting Keeper of Archaeology & Numismatics. Commissioner, Royal Commission on the Ancient and Historical Monuments of Wales.

Elizabeth A. Walker
Curator of Palaeolithic and Mesolithic Archaeology. A stone tool expert, she has worked on the excavations of numerous cave sites across Wales, including Pontnewydd Cave, and directed her own excavations on Burry Holms, Gower.

Findspots for objects (where known)

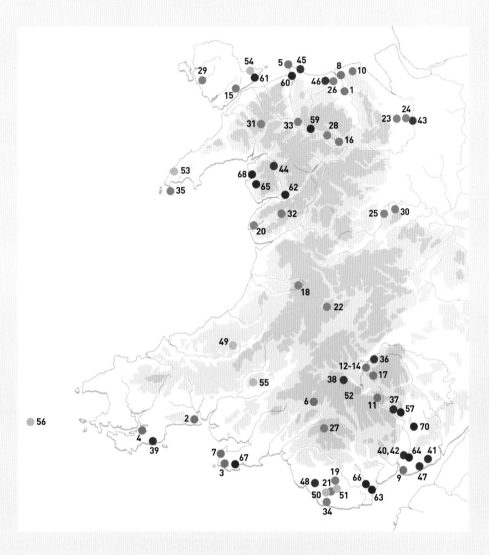

Legend:
- Palaeolithic, Mesolithic
- Neolithic
- Bronze Age
- Iron Age
- Roman
- Early Medieval
- Medieval